Taylor.

BY

DAVID R. GREAVES

*This book is dedicated to those prisoners of war who did not get back, especially those of Stalag IVa whose funerals it was the author's sad privilege to conduct.*

# Foreword

Many books have been written about the Second World War. Most of these were about the campaigns and battles and not a few about the experiences of Prisoners of War and their escapes, successful or unsuccessful. In the vast majority of cases the authors were officers and the number of personal reminiscences by NCOs or other ranks is by comparison minute.

This account by David Greaves, a corporal in an armoured regiment, covers the period from June 1942 when he was taken prisoner during the withdrawal from Cyrenaica. It includes a vivid description of a battle, the privations of prisoners in North Africa before evacuation, life in hospital and in POW camps in Italy and Czechoslavakia, and his final escape to the advancing American forces to avoid the Russians.

As somebody who underwent similar experiences, albeit in German hands and in officer camps, I found the book fascinating. Though I wasn't there, the whole story reads true, without exaggeration or unnecessary embellishment. David Greaves' spiritual growth while a POW, which ultimately led to his ordination, enabled him to take responsibilities far beyond his rank, to the comfort and benefit of his comrades.

It is a heart warming and moving tale.

Colonel K.N. Wylie. D.S.O., M.B.E.

Inside Story

First published 1989 by Capella Publications



Set in Goudy Old Style
by Capella D.T.P. Bureau
Charles Estate, Stowmarket IP14 5AH.
Printed and Bound by Short Run Press, Exeter.



ISBN 0 946 443 11 4

# Preface

Many books have been published giving accounts of some of the remarkable and courageous escapes made by prisoners of war during World War Two, and I would be the last to deny the authors of such books their right to the popularity they have enjoyed. I have read many of them myself. My hope and purpose in writing this book is to reminds present and future generations of the no less remarkable courage of those who endured with tremendous fortitude, self discipline, and often an incredible sense of humour under the most difficult circumstances, the privations and pressure of years of captivity behind barbed wire. Their unquenchable spirit and determined resistance also tied down to prison guard duties thousands of Italian and German troops who might otherwise have been available to fight in the battle for Europe.

David Greaves.

# Contents

## List of Illustrations



I am grateful to my son John who has redrawn the two line drawings from my own original somewhat crude sketches. D.R.G.

## CHAPTER ONE

# In the Bag

JUNE 13TH 1942 was not a good day! It was one of those days that one would like to forget but never will, and the events of that day are as clear in my mind today – forty-six years later – as if they had occurred yesterday. The night that followed was even worse, but then I'm jumping the gun a bit, or rather 'guns' for there were many of them. By June of that year, things were looking pretty desperate for the British army in the Western desert. The year before, we had known the exhilarating experience of chasing Rommel and his Afrika Korps all the way to Agedabia and el Agheila; but now the German counter-attack had been successfully launched. The so called 'Gazala Line' had been deeply penetrated by German armoured divisions. British armour, outgunned and lightly armoured in comparison with the German tanks, was being decimated in the bitter battle of the 'Cauldron' about ten miles south of Trigh Capuzzo. I was then a loader-operator in a Cruiser tank of the 22nd Armoured Brigade which was at this time attached to the 7th Armoured Division – the famous Desert Rats. May and early June seemed to consist of one long battle as seemingly endless formations of German tanks swept out of the desert to batter a way through to Tobruk and the coast.

The Gazala line consisted of a long defensive system of minefields and barbed wire with strongly fortified zones called 'boxes' at intervals along its length. The thinking behind the strategy seems to have been that the Germans, having located the minefields, would be forced to go round them and thus come within range of the guns of one or the other of the 'boxes' and batter themselves to pieces against the well prepared defences. Unfortunately, Rommel was far too wily a general to do any such thing. Instead, he sent his sappers to clear a couple of lanes through the minefields on either side of the 150th Infantry Brigade's box, west of the Cauldron, poured his panzers through these gaps, isolated the box and, after a bitter struggle, overwhelmed it. He next turned his attention to the Bir Hacheim box held by the Free French. This was now dealt with in the same way, and by the 9th June this too had been cut off and was under massive attack, by Stuka dive bombers from the air and on land by heavy artillery concentrations and tank and infantry assaults. The Free French fought magnificently, but all efforts by the 7th Armoured Division to break the German stranglehold failed and that box too fell.

The fall of Bir Hacheim meant that the Guards Brigade's box at 'Knightsbridge' was now threatened and already under heavy attack. Tanks of the 21st Panzer Division were in action against the 4th Armoured Brigade between el Adem and Knightsbridge. My own Brigade – the 22nd Armoured – was rushed up to assist the 4th and was given the task of keeping open an escape corridor through which the Guards and other troops in the box could be withdrawn and live to fight another day. Which brings me back to that unpleasantest of days – June 13th.

All that day we sat in a long extended line, with our tank motors silent and our guns facing towards the enemy, whilst the troops from the Knightsbridge box pulled out of danger behind us. It was a grim experience. The largest gun we mounted on our Cruiser tanks at that time was the two pounder. When one remembers that some of the German tanks were firing fourteen pound shells at us, it all seemed a little unfair! In a fast moving and noisy tank battle you could forget, temporarily, that the German tanks were more heavily armoured, had bigger guns, and – not having engines that ran on high octane petrol as ours did – caught fire less easily. Cruisers were fairly fast, thank God, had a low profile and the advantage of power driven turrets, so that in battle one could at least charge flat out at the enemy and hope to get him within the limited range of your two pounder before he got you.

None of that applied on June 13th. All day long we were sitting ducks, being shelled from positions way out of range of our guns. Every so often the gunner would call out to the tank commander “Shall I let a round off, sir?” and the tank commander would say “Might as well I suppose”. So the two pounder would be fired and we would watch the solid shot harmlessly kick up dust way off in the empty desert. The only good it did was to relieve our feelings a bit. From time to time we would listen to the swish of German shells whistling past our tank and see one or other of our neighbours go up in smoke. So it continued all day and the number of surviving tanks got less and less, but still we sat there, waiting for the radio order that would tell us we could withdraw.

Night really does ‘fall’ in the desert – there is very little twilight. When darkess fell – except where knocked out tanks were blazing – we were still in position. Out in the darkness before us we were acutely aware that a great deal else was going on! We could hear the rumble of vehicle motors – tanks and lorries – the clanking of tank tracks, even the sound of voices as the noises got nearer. But our orders were plain: no withdrawal until the order was given. At about midnight, it came. The Guards Brigade had been safely evacuated from the Knightsbridge box and we could now withdraw ourselves from what had obviously become a very dangerous position. The order was given “Start up” and at once the tank engines roared into life and we prepared to move off. However, as soon as the engines started up, every kind of star shell, Verey light and flare went up from the German lines and by the light of them we could see that under cover of darkness the German troops had moved up to form a tight, and all too close, semi-circle around us – some near enough for us to see the reflection of the star shells on their helmets! They opened up with everything they had got, which was considerable, and immediately there were tanks and vehicles burning all around us.

My tank was hit in the first salvo. There was a horrible ‘thump’ in the engine, which stopped dead. Petrol fumes began to seep into the turret. My usual Tank Commander, a Captain from the 3rd County of London Yeomanry, had been wounded by shrapnel from an airburst a few days earlier and had been sent off to hospital. His place had been taken by a young officer (who shall be nameless!) straight out from O.C.T.U. and for whom this was no doubt his first taste of battle. When the tank was hit, this young officer shouted out to the rest of the crew: “You stay here

– I'll go and get a tow." The rest of us could hardly believe our ears! Here we were, sitting in what had suddenly become a large incendiary bomb due to explode any minute, machine gun bullets rattling like hail on the outside of the turret – and he was proposing to go and get a tow! I felt sure that he must have been either quite mad, or very brave. To this day I've never been able to decide which! Anyway, we sat tight, as ordered, while he clambered out of the top of the turret – somehow, by a miracle, without being hit – and ran over to one of the few remaining tanks that were still able to move and was about to make a dash out of the holocaust, and asked for a tow! The answer he got I cannot begin to imagine, but it must have been something like "Don't be a bloody fool – jump on the back!", for that at any rate is what he did. The last we saw of our tank commander he was clinging for dear life on the back of one of the escaping tanks as it tore off into the darkness.

As second in command, that left me, with the exalted rank of two stripes and a crown, to decide what to do next – and those stripes only meant a Lance Corporal in my Regiment![1] I had few doubts about what needed to be done. The tank was obviously likely to 'brew up' at any moment, so I ordered the rest of the crew to bale out at once. British tanks were oddly designed at that time, in that the only way out was through the top of the turret, which meant that you had to expose your whole body to enemy fire! However, again by some miracle we all managed to get out safely, and using the tank as cover began to crawl away towards the darkness beyond the area which was now brilliantly illuminated by blazing tanks and other vehicles. It was just as well that we got clear when we did. A few moments after we had baled out of it our tank blew up and was soon adding its own illumination and – with exploding ammunition – danger, to the scene.

The next ten minutes or so were a nightmare. The Germans knew that there might be tank crews and other troops trying to make their escape and were sweeping the whole area with machine-gun fire. In spite of the light from the burning vehicles around, the tracer bullets they were firing were clearly visible and we could see their fiery 'hoses' crossing and criss-crossing the desert sands just a foot or so above ground level. Whenever we saw one of these 'bullet streams' snaking towards us

1 The Middlesex Yeomanry

we all froze and flattened ourselves as much as we could on the sand as we felt the windage of it pass over us, and hoped the German gunner wouldn't hiccup or sneeze at that precise moment. If he did, we'd be dead! Just when we were beginning to hope we'd got clear, the gunner (from the 2nd Royal Gloucestershire Hussars) who was crawling beside me screamed out "I've been hit – I've been hit." When this happened, the driver got to his feet and ran off towards the darkness and we never saw him again. That left just me and the badly wounded gunner, sobbing with pain, lying beside me. I asked him if he thought he could still crawl. He said he would try. So the two of us set off again, though much more slowly now, into the darkness beyond, away from the light of the blazing vehicles behind us.

After what seemed hours – they were probably only minutes – we came across a slit trench that somebody, whether English or German we neither knew nor cared, had dug in the desert sand. Very thankfully we crawled into it. It gave us immediate protection from the machine gunning of course, but when I tried to do something about my companion's wounds, there was a new problem. While it was still almost as light as day up on the surface, it was pitch dark down in the slit trench and I could not see enough to tell how badly wounded he was. In fact, as I felt his leg he appeared to have a series of holes down it and was obviously losing a great deal of blood. I only had the one field dressing carried by all soldiers at that time so I tied that as tightly as I could around the topmost wound but could do nothing about the others. Thankfully, for his sake, we were not there for very long. The Germans must have seen us go to ground, because a few moments later a truck load of German soldiers, brandishing all kinds of unpleasant looking stick grenades and machine pistols drove straight up to our slit trench shouting "Hands up". We were prisoners.

The men of the 21st Panzer Division turned out to be very different from the Germans I was to meet later in Nazi Germany. They treated us very much as we would have treated them. We were both given a cigarette ('Players', I noticed!) – an indication of N.A.A.F.I. stores captured in various British Army Dumps they had overrun on their advance – and a mug of tea. A German officer offered us both a blanket to wrap ourselves in, for which we were very grateful. It was bitterly cold in the desert at about three o'clock in the morning. We had baled out in our khaki shorts and shirts, which, after our recent exertions, were wet with cold and clammy sweat. My wounded companion was feeling the cold far worse than I was. Partly because of loss of blood, and partly, no doubt, as a result of shock and pain, he was now shivering and trembling like a man with malaria, so I put his own blanket over his chest and shoulders, and wrapped mine round his legs and feet, as any soldier would have done. Some little while later the German Officer returned with an ambulance (also British, though now with German markings!) to pick up the wounded man. He first glanced, and then glared at me when he saw that I no longer had the blanket he had given me, but then as the German stretcher bearers got out of the ambulance to lift my companion on to a stretcher, he saw where both the blankets were and came over to me. To my surprise he put his hand on my shoulder, smiled at me like some fond uncle and said "*Gute soldaten!*" and strode off looking, I thought, a little embarrassed. I've often wondered if he survived the war. I rather hope so!

A young Feldwebel[1] then handed me another blanket and indicated that I should lie down by his nearby truck and go to sleep. I felt drained and exhausted by now and would gladly have done so, but the departure of my companion in the ambulance to some Advanced Dressing Station left me as the sole prisoner in that part of the German front that night. The result was that as the German tanks came back into their *laager*[2] the tank crews kept coming over to see their prize exhibit! It was all very matey. They would bring out photos of their wives and sweethearts. Those who could speak English – and many could – would ask how long I thought the war would last? how did the bombing of London compare with the bombing the R.A.F. was doing in Germany? and other similar questions. Eventually I was left in peace and finally dropped off to sleep. Not for long. Before dawn the Feldwebel prodded me with his foot and said "*aufstehen* – today you will take part in a German advance!" He was quite right, I did. The 21st Panzer Division moved up to begin the German attack on Tobruk. Unwillingly, I went with them.

1 A German non-commissioned rank for which there is no exact equivalent in British Army ranks. Probably Company Sergeant-Major would be about the nearest.

2 Used by both British and German forces to denote a vehicle assembly area.

## CHAPTER TWO

# Suani-ben-Adem to Capua

TOBRUK FELL two days later. Large numbers of British, South African and Indian soldiers were taken prisoner – far too many for the Africa Korps to cope with in the rapidly moving front line – so a convoy of big German trucks came up to carry the prisoners of war back across Cyrenaica and into Tripolitania, away from the fighting. That long trek was itself a trying experience, but far worse was to come. Each day, before first light, we were loaded up into the trucks under the watchful eyes of German guards and the muzzles of the machine guns of escorting armoured cars. We then bumped and rocked our way all day through the blinding dust of the lorries in front of us, in the blistering heat of the desert sun, without a break. As night fell we would be herded into some wire 'cage' where, if we were lucky, we might be given a tin of German bully beef – or was it horse?. Sometimes a water truck would be backed up to the barbed wire so that we could fill our hands, tin hats – if we still had them – or mess tins to get a drink. The next day would be the same, and the next, and the next. Derna, Barce, Benghazi, Agedabia, Sirte, Homs – the journey seemed endless. At last we were herded into yet another wire cage and the guards (Italian and Senussi now, no longer German) told us we were at Suani-ben-Adem. They also told us that we would only be there a few days and then we would be shipped across the Mediterranean to Sicily and on to proper P.o.W. camps in Italy. Conditions were pretty ghastly. It was just an area of soft, desert sand surrounded by barbed wire – no huts, not even tents – and the only latrine was a long open trench with a pole lashed to two uprights across it in lieu of a lavatory seat. We were each given a blanket to lie down on and wrap ourselves in at night. Food was in short supply and barely edible. It consisted of square, hard, ship's biscuits which were full of weevils and their repulsive looking grubs, and a small round tin of meat a day. But we weren't too worried – we could stand it for a few days. That was in June 1942. We were still there in November! By then the number of men in the camp had at least trebled. Sidi Barrani had fallen, so had Mersa Matruh, Fuka and Daba. Almost every day more lorry loads of prisoners were herded into the already overcrowded cage. The khaki shirts and shorts we had been captured in, way back in June, were by now verminous and filthy rags. We had neither washed nor shaved for six months and the soft desert sand crawled with myriads of lice and fleas. If you had to walk across the camp, perhaps to visit the stinking, overflowing latrine trench, when you got there your first instinctive action would be to put both hands on your knees and run your hands down to your feet to wipe off all you could of the mass of fleas and lice that by then would be crawling up them. At night there was *no* escape. You had to lie down on that sand, wrap yourself in your filthy and verminous blanket and feel the wretched hordes swarming all over your body. By now (though unknown to us), the British Army was at the beginning of its victorious breakthrough from Alamein. The Royal Navy was blockading the Mediterranean with all the submarines and ships that it could muster, to prevent reinforcements getting through to Rommel along his already over extended supply lines. Food became even more scarce and constant hunger made us weak and ill and open to all kinds of infections. Many of the vermin bites on our ankles, legs , and arms turned into great festering sores, sometimes an inch or more across. To add to the problem, dysentery was rife – the result no doubt of the bluebottles and flies that swarmed around the open sewer of the latrine, then crowded round your mouth and on your food whenever you had anything to eat! When the weather got colder – as it does in the desert in November, particularly at night – men started to go down with pneumonia, bronchitis and various other chest complaints. It was in that month that the first deaths occurred in the camp. Many others knew that without medical attention very soon they too would be dying, for you couldn't go on living for long when even the meagre food you were given just went straight through you in a matter of minutes. Life seemed to have reached rock bottom.

I will return to events in this hell camp of Suani-ben-Adem later in the narrative, because it was certain experiences that I had there that were to change my life completely and really supply my reason for writing it, but they all tie up with later events, so I will continue for now. Towards the end of the month we were suddenly ordered to leave the camp and were marched – or rather, we shambled – off to Tripoli docks and were taken on board an Italian freighter. We were stowed away in the hold of the ship, so tightly packed that you could only sit with your knees drawn up and pressed against somebody's back, while someone else had their knees stuck into your own. It was almost totally dark once the hatches were put back over us but the ship's crew had cheered us by saying that soon we would be in Sicily, and the day after in Italy. In spite of the griping pains of our dysentery we felt quite elated at the thought that we had seen the last of Suani-ben-Adem and would almost gladly put up with the discomfort of one or two nights in the ship's hold.

It didn't quite turn out to be as easy as that. The Royal Navy's blockade was too good. We set sail that night as the crew had said we would, but after an hour or two of sailing – I had no means of telling how long it was and in any case was really too ill to care – there was a submarine scare, and we turned back. The same thing happened the next night, and the next. I lost all sense of time and I suspect may have been semi-conscious part of it. It seemed like an eternity. Someone afterwards told me that it was six days and nights before we finally reached Sicily. That I cannot be sure of. All I do remember is that when the hatches were lifted off and those of us who could still stand were helped out and led on to the shore, it was pouring with rain and seemed much colder than I had expected Sicily to be. I shall never forget the looks of both horror and pity on the faces of the open mouthed Sicilian women who stood in the streets and watched us shambling by, gaunt, unshaven and dirty, wrapped still, against the cold, in our filthy, ragged blankets, as we were taken off to the railway station, there to be loaded, appropriately enough, into cattle-trucks – because I'm sure that's what we smelt like

– to be taken across Sicily. I imagine that we must have looked a bit like prisoners from Belsen or Auschwitz.

After an uncomfortable but uneventful journey across Sicily, we were put on board another boat bound this time for Italy. This was a very much more pleasant trip across the narrow Messina Straits, – filled with the Italian Navy, I remember – because this time we were allowed to remain on deck. Once on shore we were again put into cattle trucks and after quite a long journey we arrived at a huge transit camp at Capua. Here all the prisoners were examined by a team of doctors, not only Italian but British and South African army doctors, who though themselves prisoners of war, were being used to assist in this way. I was examined first by a South African doctor who then referred me to an Italian doctor to confirm that I was a hospital case. With a bunch of other prisoners I was sent off to Casserta Hospital near Naples, where I was soon put into a bed in one of the wards, a notice hanging at the foot of it stating that I had chronic bronchitis, pleurisy, dysentry, yellow jaundice, various desert sores and ulcers, and that my weight was six and a half stones. It had been a near thing!

CHAPTER THREE

# Caserta Hospital

THIS WAS HEAVEN! No doubt compared with any modern hospital wartime Caserta hospital would be considered primitive in the extreme. The Italian staff had very little in the way of medical supplies and not enough bed linen to comply with today's standards of hygiene and patient care, but just to have washed all over and to be in a real bed with sheets and a pillow seemed like heaven after all the privations of Suani-ben-Adem. There was still the Italian military guard with his rifle and bayonet on the landing outside the ward and, if no longer regiments of fleas to contend with, there were still plenty of bed bugs to share your bed at night and even the odd louse or two. But the nuns who were the nursing sisters in charge of the wards made up for all such petty annoyances. They were true angels of mercy, sweet and gentle with the patients, but at times holy terrors, in the truest sense, to the Italian orderlies who scuttled about to do whatever the *sorella* ordered them. There was a large crucifix above the door in each ward and when Sister first entered each morning she would stop, bow her head and with hands pressed demurely together say a long prayer (so rapidly I could never tell whether it was in Latin or Italian) but having concluded with "Amen" she would raise her head and with blazing eyes and a mouth open like a letter box she would stride down the ward screaming out a string of staccato orders emphasized by a finger jabbing in different directions as startled orderlies hurried to open windows that had been kept firmly shut all night, straighten beds, or pick up articles that had been carelessly dropped on the floor. They were marvellous! On more than one occasion I saw one of these nuns come into the ward carrying a daintily cooked omelette. This would be at considerable risk to herself, for it was *streng verboten*, as far as the German authorities were concerned, to supplement a prisoner's diet in any way, or indeed, for a civilian even to possess an egg. Yet the nun would come in and sit by some British lad's bed and try to spoon feed him – often in the quite forlorn hope that he might somehow be able to retain some nourishment, in a digestive system that had already been completely destroyed by dysentery – long enough to keep him alive. Having done her best, and failed, she would sit with him and hold his hand and pray over him until he died.

Because I had dysentery I was on a 'no fat' diet which simply meant that I had either rice or macaroni, boiled in water with no oil, puree, or anything else added. It was a bit like eating glue. But perhaps it had a similar effect because gradually, and sometimes painfully, the griping and the constant 'runs' began to cease and I even began to put on a bit of weight. I was rather peeved at Christmas time though, when most of the patients in the ward were given a special Christmas Red Cross Food Parcel which I wasn't allowed because of my no fat diet. It seemed hard at the time, but I am sure it was really the right decision.

The bronchitis and pleurisy took a good deal longer to clear up, probably because there was little in the way of medicine. I used to get regular needle jabs in my backside, administered with a true Italian flourish by an orderly who I suspected may have been a knife thrower in a circus before his military callup – judging by his style with a hypodermic syringe. I think they were mostly doses of vitamin supplements. My chest must have become quite well known among Italian medical student circles. I got thoroughly fed up with the very frequent visits of a rather pompous looking Italian medical officer who must have been a chest specialist, I suppose. He used to march straight down the ward to my bed, followed by one of the Sisters and a large group of students. They would then all gather round; I would be ordered to sit up and to remove my hospital night shirt, and then under instructions from the specialist, all the students would take turns to hold a coin against various places on my chest and to hit it – the coin, that is! – with a second coin, while the rest took turns to listen with a stethoscope held at my back. There was no heating in the ward and even in southern Italy it could sometimes be pretty chilly at that time of the year. I can only hope that my chest added something to the world's medical knowledge.

One of the most important events which took place during my stay at Caserta was the visit made to the hospital by a representative from the Vatican. This resulted in two things. First, I was able to send off a pre-printed card which my parents eventually received and which told them that I was a prisoner of war and not wounded. It was a great relief to them to receive this, as up to that moment I had simply been reported missing for the previous six months. The second thing that I much appreciated was that the kindly old priest who came round the ward presented to each P.o.W. a Christmas gift from the Vatican. It was a little notebook with a calendar for the year and a brief selection of Christmas carols at the back. There were quotations from Papal speeches on each page, but there was also plenty of room for one's own notes and jottings, and since I already had a burning desire to begin making some sort of record of the things I saw going on around me, I was very grateful and took the first opportunity that came along to purloin a pencil from one of the orderlies. So began a diary that was to cover the next three years of my life. Little did I know then that it was to accompany me from Italy into Germany, up into Czechoslovakia and back across Germany and France home to England. Though battered and travel-stained, it is still with me.

Eventually, having reached the great weight of eight stone, I was declared fit to be discharged from hospital. Together with a dozen or so more, I was taken off to the nearest railway station under guard, put on a train bound for Porto San Giorgio and on from there to a Prisoner of War Camp – Campo P.G. 70, near Fermo.

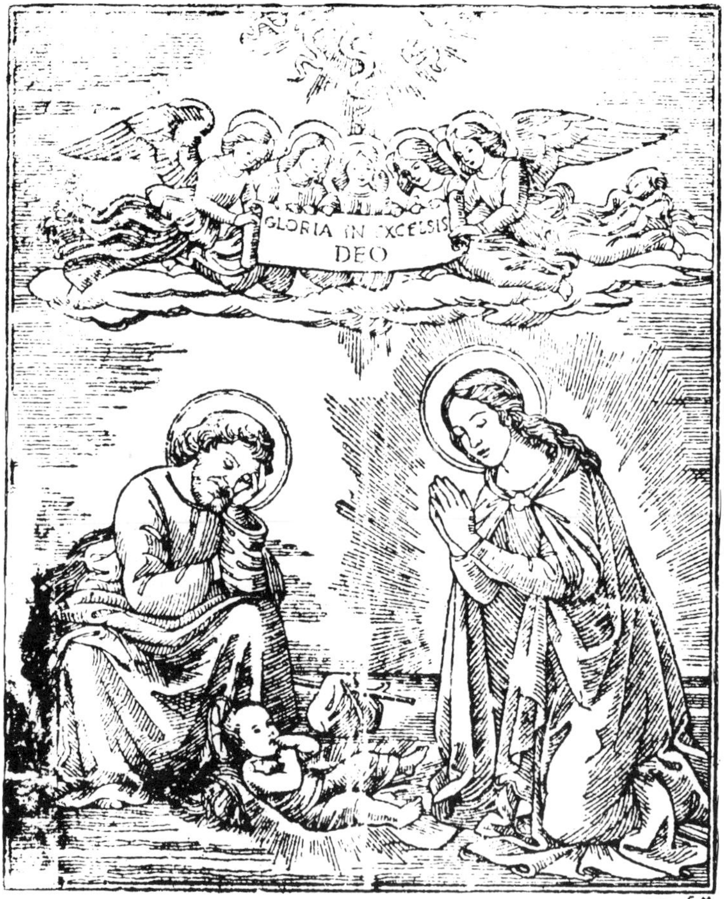

FROM THE VATICAN PICTURE GALLERY

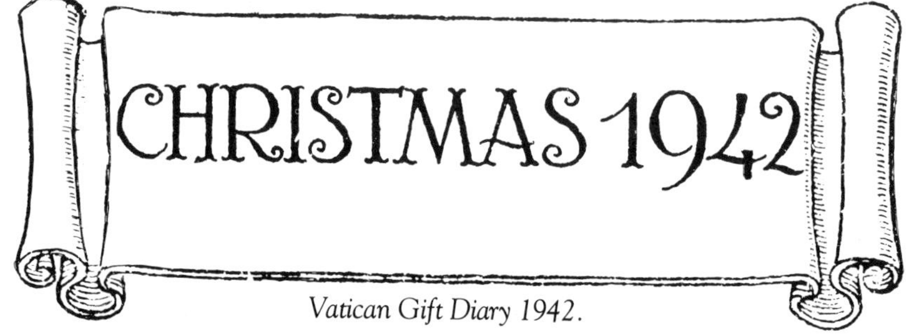


*Vatican Gift Diary 1942.*

Mod. 40

CHRISTMAS GREETINGS

SECRETARIAT OF STATE
TO HIS HOLINESS

PASSED
P.W. 2890

Date 24 Nov 1942

Sender GREAVES DAVID REGINALD

Rank L/CPL No. 2580648

Camp No. 66 Military Post 3400

Town MUSWELL HILL

County LONDON N.10

Country ENGLAND

Message (10 words - Season's greetings only)

BEST WISHES FOR CHRISTMAS
AND NEW YEAR
FROM
DAVE

*Christmas Greetings card sent from Caserta hospital.*

My dear, Mother & Dad.

(post mark date)
(*Data del timbro postale*)

I am alright (I have not been wounded (or) ~~I have been slightly wounded~~). I am a prisoner of the Italians and I am being treated well.
Sto bene (non sono stato ferito (o) sono stato ferito leggermente). Sono stato catturato dagli Italiani e mi trovo bene.

Shortly I shall be transferred to a prisoner's camp and I will let you have my new address.
Nei prossimi giorni sarò trasferito in un campo di prigionieri del quale vi comunicherò l'indirizzo.

Only then I will be able to receive letters from you and to reply.
Soltanto allora potrò ricevere la vostra corrispondenza e rispondervi.

David. R. Greaves.
(signature)
(firma)

With love David.
Saluti affettuosi

*Red Cross Postcard.*

## CHAPTER FOUR

# The Place of the Mulberry Trees

FROM THE DISTANCE P.G.70 looked more like an industrial site than a prison camp. It was dominated by four large concrete warehouses resembling huge bunkers, but there was also the greenness of plenty of trees that softened the harshness of the grey buildings. It was only as we got nearer that we began to see the barbed wire fence all round it, the machine gun towers overlooking it, and the Italian troops – a whole battalion of them – encamped around the perimeter. We were to learn that it had indeed been an industrial site before the war. The large warehouses had been used mainly for storing silk – hence the many mulberry trees we had seen from a distance – but also, I believe, flax and fruit. As we arrived at the gate it was opened by a guard and we were handed over to the senior British Warrant Officer in the Camp. Telling us to follow him, he led us to one of the great warehouses. Stepping inside from the bright sunlight it seemed so dark that at first I could not see a thing. There were no windows, except some very small ones high up at the top the grey walls. Then, as my eyes adjusted to the gloom, my first impression was that it was rather like looking at a wood-ants' nest that someone had kicked open to reveal swarms of ants running in all directions. As far as my eyes could focus there stretched down the building long narrow corridors formed by rows of wooden three-tiered bunks arranged in pairs back to back. Everywhere you looked there were bodies, some lying prone on beds, some sitting on beds, some hurrying to and fro between the beds. The babel of sound was deafening! I was led to a bed in the middle of one of the three tier bunks, told that this was to be mine, that I should dump whatever belongings I might have there and report to the stores to draw a straw filled palliasse and a blanket. These would cover the wooden slats of what was now to be not just my bed but my *lebensraum*, or living space. There I would sleep by night, sit to eat my food by day and retire to when I wanted to be by myself – only you could never be by yourself. Talk about privacy – there was none! Your brother man was above and below you, if you were in a middle bunk, and all around you on every side, whether you liked it or not. I have never again experienced such 'close fellowship' as there was in P.G.70! There were about seven thousand men in that camp.

Life there was very much what you made it. We were not made to work, as we were later in Germany. There were no parades, except when there were special announcements to be made, or when the Italian guards wanted to make their periodic searches for knives and other weapons, escape equipment, or the hidden radio they knew we had because the B.B.C. news was read out in each block every day. In one sense this was good, but it had very real psychological dangers too, because it meant that if a man wanted to, he could simply lie on his bunk and withdraw into himself completely and do nothing. He could become so detached from life that he might not even bother to leave his bed to draw what meagre rations there were, and unless someone could help him snap out of it, he would be dead a week later. We called it 'barbed-wire-itis' and, believe me, it could be a killer. On the other hand, in a camp with that number of men in it, there would always be men from all walks of life and with many different interests, so it was not long before former school teachers were holding classes on all kinds of subjects, interest lectures were held, a camp choir came into being, an orchestra formed, and I found myself cast as a 'gnome' in the enchanted wood scene of *The Wicked Witch of Wonderland*! This was a pantomime we produced for all the camp, and written by one of the prisoners. Music was selected for the orchestra – mostly from the current 'hits' but sung to quite unprintable words! Carpenters and other craftsmen had made what looked to us very professional and effective scenery from the plywood cases in which the Red Cross food parcels were packed and from bed boards and other scrounged bits of wood, cardboard and cloth. A team of artists, some ex-art teachers, commercial artists and other professionals, painted it. Electricians and radio mechanics formed a team to attend to the lighting and special effects. Hundreds of cigarettes, the main currency in use between the prisoners and the Italian guards, changed hands through the wire to obtain almost everything needed to

*P.G.70 Pantomime "Gnomes"*

put on the show. The enchanted wood scene was to be performed in very dim lighting so that the luminous paint on the ghostly looking trees and the special electrical effects would glow more brightly. The only trouble was that the costumes for the six gnomes were not finished in time for rehearsals and we put them on for the first time on the night of the performance. The result of that was, well, disastrous for the gnomes –

hilarious for the audience! In fact it brought the house down and some of the scenery as well.

The idea was that the gnomes would do a simple little dance routine – well practised in rehearsals – to suitable 'gnomish' music. The costumes consisted of large tubes of thick paper on wire frames, about four feet long, with handles on the inside to hold them up. On the front of each tube was painted a large smiling face; on the back a fearsome, scowling face. Beneath each tube protruded white and very skinny bare legs. As we danced and hopped around the stage, sometimes we showed a smiling face to the audience, sometimes a scowling one – all simple and straightforward in theory. In practice it was rather less simple. The trouble was that once you had got the tube over your head you very quickly discovered that no way could you move – let alone dance – and hold the tube steady enough to see through the tiny little eye holes that had been made in the front of the costume. One reverse hop and the gnomes were lost! Helplessly the six ridiculous little figures, with their sparrow-like legs sticking out at the bottom of each tube, staggered about the stage, cannoned into each other, demolished scenery, or fell completely off the stage into the orchestra! The audience, including some of the Italian guards, were reduced to an equal state of helplessness as they doubled up and rolled about with laughter. It was a riproaring success!

Another activity I began at this time was the writing of doggerel verse – I cannot presume to call it poetry – about various aspects of P.o.W. life, using of course the note book I had been given while in Caserta Hospital. They were nearly all on the subject of food. Although better fed than in Libya, we were still always hungry and indeed I doubt whether many of us would have survived were it not for the Red Cross food parcels that reached us fairly regularly from England, Scotland and Canada. The only hot 'meal' we received was a sort of vegetable soup; I say "sort of" because I could never decide what the vegetable was! It looked rather like dandelions to me, but was probably some kind of greens. Whatever it was, quite obviously nobody ever bothered to wash it before throwing it into the cooking pots because there were always snails, slugs, beetles and caterpillars and grubs of all kinds floating on the top! Occasionally we were told there was supposed to be some meat in it, though this was usually conspicuous by its absence, and it should have been thickened with rice, but that had often been sold off on the black market long before it could reach the pot. Still, it was warm and didn't taste too bad and it was better than nothing, so we dutifully queued up in our groups – I was in group 91 – for our ladleful. We called it "skilly".

*Skilly*

Weeds and water, warm and wet
A guinea pig eats more, I'll bet!
Still, the taste can be quite nice
– "has anybody seen the rice?!"
The meat is in , or so they say,
And ninety one's on first today.
"I'll say the meat's in," someone wails
"I've more than my fair share of snails!"
The next group's pot's as thick as mortar!
Ours consists of chiefly water.
Most of us think the cook's to blame
For why shouldn't ours be just the same?
O roll on the day, and may it be soon,
when we'll use knifes and forks
And not just a spoon!

The other food that we received from the Italians was the bread ration. This was a small round loaf of coarse brown bread – about the size of a doughnut – which was brought up from the 'magazine', or Q.M. Store, in the adjoining military camp each evening. Once you had received your small loaf, you used an old razor blade to cut it up into as many slices as possible – and it was truly amazing how many slices some were able to get out of one small loaf! But then, you see, you could adopt a sort of millionaire attitude to life. You could say to yourself "I think I'll have four slices for supper tonight – and perhaps two or three for breakfast – and eat the rest with the skilly for lunch!" Small though it was, it was good solid food, and if once in a while because of air-raids or transport breakdowns, the bread ration did not arrive, you went to bed that night feeling just that bit more hungry and depressed. No wonder that towards evening there would always be a little knot of anxious prisoners peering through the barbed-wire of the gate at the Camp entrance looking out for the bread lorry climbing up the hill towards us. We called it:

*The Wee Brown Bun*

How patiently we watch and wait,
Getting as close as we can to the gate;
Somebody says it was actually seen
to be carried into the magazine.
Others say, no, it's not in yet,
The first one's willing to take a bet!
In reality nobody knows what's what,
Whether it's really in or not!
But listen! I hear a mighty cheer
And a voice rings out both loud and clear,
"Will group commanders please draw bread"
So we'll eat before we to bed!
Hurray! the Bread's in.

I have already mentioned the importance of the Red Cross food parcels to us. I really do believe that they made just the difference that kept body and soul together and I am sure that I and many other ex-P.o.W.s will be eternally grateful to the British and Canadian Red Cross Societies for them. They were supposed to be distributed, one for each prisoner, every week. Mostly that is what happened, but again, occasionally, for reasons we could not know, the parcels did not arrive and life became at once that much more intolerable. When they did come however they precipitated another problem. The British parcels often had in them things like egg powder and bacon. The Scottish parcels always contained porage oats, and who wants to eat raw bacon or spoon dry porage oats?! Here was a dilemma: the possession of matches and the lighting of fires was forbidden, so what could poor hungry prisoners do about it? In adversity the British soldier simply refuses to be beaten – he finds a way round these minor difficulties. The obvious happened – a fire was lit in the middle of the camp. How, I don't know, but probably with the help of somebody's spectacle lens and the Italian sunshine. Immediately the

Italian guards rushed in with rifles at the ready and stamped it out. But before they could get to the other side of the wire, another fire was burning somewhere else and they came rushing back to deal with that. After the performance had been repeated several times they gave up, and a part of the centre of the Camp soon became known by English and Italians alike as 'the brewing patch'.

To make use of the brewing patch you needed a brewing stove. These were made from the sides of the empty tins from the Red Cross Parcels stamped out flat and joined together. The large 'Klim' (milk spelt backwards!) powdered milk tins, an older generation may remember, were very useful for this. From these, and other bits of scrap metal, all kinds of ingenious mini-ovens were designed and made. Some even had little handles you turned to make a fan wheel revolve under your fire, so that you could obtain the maximum amount of heat from the minimum amount of fuel, scraps of cardboard, twigs from the trees or the odd chip of wood removed from somebody else's bed board! Armed with your brewing stove and whatever you planned to cook, you strode off into the smoke of the brewing patch and cried out "any embers?" At any time of day or night there would be fires burning and, like the Olympic flame, once ignited, the fire was never allowed to go out. After a while a voice would answer through the smoke: "here you are, chum", and someone who had completed his cooking would tip the embers of his fire into your stove; you would add your bits of paper and wood, fan it into a flame and get on with your cooking. By the time you had finished other voices would be crying out: "any embers?"

Here are two poems, one about the brewing patch, the other in praise of Red Cross parcels:

### *Any Embers*

Scarce has the sound, as of a dying duck[1]
That is reveille died away,
Forth from the barrack-room to try his luck
The early brewer sings his morning lay,
"Any Embers?"

And all day long the scents of brewing rise
And every day continues through the week,
And ever from the smoke ring out the cries
Of those with empty brewing fires who seek
"Any Embers?"

Some try their hand at egg-flakes, some burgoo[2]
Some fry up sausages or galantine
The scent of frying onions rises too
And fresh fires start to burn where there have been
"Any Embers?"

God grant that as the swallow year by year
Comes back to build anew beneath the eaves
We may return to those we hold so dear
And stamp the fires of hatred out, nor leave
"Any Embers?"

### *Parcel Morning*

How cheerfully we wake and rise
How warm the sun, how clear the skies!
For this is the best day of the week,
This is the day on which we EAT!
On Parcel Morning

---

1 My apologies to Scottish readers, but I must explain that reveille in this camp was played on the bag-pipes, the noise of which, at 0600, would turn even a haggis into a Sassenach!

2 Army slang for porridge.

Once we took food without giving a thought,
All that we fancied we went out and bought.
Once we believed that we ate to live,
Now we enjoy what the Red Cross give
On parcel Morning.

What have you got? A "London Y"?[3]
With a smashing fig pudding and Cornish pie,
We touched for Scottish, with jam in it too,
Let's hurry back for we must have a brew
On Parcel Morning.

Split up the biscuits, chocolate and jam,
What's that – it's raining? We don't give a damn!
For the tea's on the boil and laid out on the bed
We've a pudding and biscuits and jam – what a spread!
On Parcel Morning.

And so grateful prisoner, just stop to think,
If parcels should cease wouldn't your spirits sink.
So just say a prayer with due reverence and piety
For that blessing, the British Red Cross Society,
On Parcel Morning

As I've already said, all the poems were about food, and as a commentary about that, I have recorded in my notebook just under that poem, the entry: 'Weighed 2-6-43 – 8 stone 5lb.' I had been over 11 stone a year before!

3 A very popular type of food parcel.

## CHAPTER FIVE

# 'P.P.s' and 'Three Gs'

Many of us who were captured in the desert in 1942 had already been away from our homes and families for two years or more. Being prisoners behind barbed wire made our sense of being cut off from loved ones all the harder to bear. During that period when we were being held in transit camps – six months in my case – it was not possible either to write or to receive letters, and all that my parents knew was that I was missing. After my discharge from Casserta Hospital and my arrival at Campo P.G.70 however, it became possible not only to write and to receive letters, but also parcels from home. These personal parcels, or 'P.P.s' as they were known, were tremendously important for our morale. Naturally enough our first letter home usually included requests for things like a razor and shaving soap, tooth brush and toothpaste, a towel, soap, flannel and other items we had been without since the day of our capture, and the eventual arrival of these in our first P.P. from home certainly helped to make us feel better – and smell a bit sweeter! Obviously all incoming parcels were opened by the Italians and anything considered unsuitable for prisoners to have, such as matches, open razors, and anything that was deemed to be useable as a weapon, was removed. The covers of books were usually ripped off – to ensure that there were no concealed files or maps or any other escape material – but in the main the treatment of the prisoners' private mail was in accordance with Geneva Conventions and handled very correctly both in Italy and, later in Germany.

Once we had received the more necessary items, P.P.s tended to contain the unexpected, and consequently were always opened with the sort of excited anticipation usually associated with birthday presents or Christmas parcels. Most young men smoked in those days, in blissful ignorance of any harmful effects it might have, so cigarettes or pipe tobacco were almost always included. Well wrapped chocolate might sometimes arrive in an edible state, but might equally well be found to have melted and soaked away into a new pair of socks. Food of any kind, in fact, didn't travel too well unless it was tinned, and even then, since the tin would probably be punctured in order that its contents might be checked, it was likely to have leaked out over everything else, or to have 'gone off'. I can remember on one occasion opening a "P.P." from my mother which contained, among other things, a home baked cake and some cigarettes. The cake, though wrapped in foil, was covered with long, green whiskers of mould and quite inedible, whilst the cigarettes all tasted like cake!. We smoked them nonetheless.

When the mail arrived in the camp the bugler sounded the usual Army 'Mail' call and we would all hurry to our respective block-houses or huts to wait for one of the sergeants – usually Sergeant Haig – to read out the names of those who could report to the gate leading to the office block to collect a parcel or letter. The signal for the gate to be opened would be three 'G's blown by the bugler.

In the next poem I tried to express something of the excitement and pleasure all mail from home, but especially a parcel, gave to us. The mention of the saxophonist is a reference to the fact that this man, who played a saxophone in the camp orchestra, must have had a large and very caring family because, – lucky man – every time mail arrived he seemed to get a parcel!

*'P.P.'s*

Suddenly a voice shouts, "Quiet please, –
the following Groups have got P.P.s."
Let's hope there's one for me or you,
But listen! he shouted "Ninety-two"
At any rate we're on the list,
It's probably one for the saxophonist!

There go the sergeants off at a run,
We'll soon know who's the lucky one,
Sergeant Haig is coming this way,
I wonder what he's got to say?
What's that Sarge? There's one for me!
Hurray! I wonder what it's going to be –
Books or fags or a 'next of kin'
With stacks and stacks of chocolate in?
But now, away to the gate I go
I mustn't be late when the three Gs blow!
There goes the bugle; I'm through the gate
Oh do hurry up, I can hardly wait!
If only the folks at home could see
The thrill that their parcel is giving me.
But when we've seen the last of war
And I am back at home once more,
I hope my life will show them clearly
My thanks – and that I love them dearly.

CHAPTER SIX

# Introducing the Padre

THERE WERE FOUR PADRES IN P.G. 70. though one, an Anglican Chaplain, the Rev. Ogilvy, was a very sick man when he arrived in the Camp and could do very little in the way of ministering to the men. He was repatriated quite early on, and although his place was taken eventually by a New Zealand Anglican, Padre Willis, by the time of his arrival most prisoners had got used to having just two who remained with us throughout. Padre Wilfred Coates, a Roman Catholic priest, looked after the 550 Catholics in the camp. Padre Douglas Thompson[1] looked after the rest. Douglas was a giant of a man, spiritually, though physically he was of quite small stature. A Padre with the Territorial Battalion of the Essex Regiment, he had been a Methodist missionary in China before the war but had come back to be commissioned into the Royal Army Chaplains' Department in 1940. He had been badly wounded before he was captured near Daba in the Western desert, and had been told by the German doctor who examined him that he would die. Thankfully that diagnosis was wrong and he survived to become 'the Padre' to thousands of prisoners in that camp and, I'm sure, in later ones.

He was a man of tireless energy and tremendous compassion. He was also, besides being a dedicated minister of the Gospel, a psychologist of considerable ability and was constantly on the lookout for cases of 'barbed-wire-itis' and various other mental and psychological states

1 Padre Thompson wrote two books about his own experiences, *Captives to Freedom* and *A Mountain Road*. In both, the author of this book is mentioned.

brought on by the frustrations and privations of captivity. Among the 'general interest' lectures run in the camp, Douglas gave talks on China, had a class of men learning to speak Chinese, and in a camp of seven thousand men – not a woman in sight – ran a very popular course on 'Marriage Preparation'!

He started a small class for men who felt that they wanted to learn more about the Christian faith, about the Bible and about prayer. Because of certain experiences I had had in the earlier days of captivity, I had become convinced that if life in that prison camp was going to have any real meaning for me I would have to look for it at a much deeper level than I had before. I found myself drawn into that class. Every morning a group consisting of Douglas Thompson, Ray Davey (who later was to found the Corremeela Community in Northern Ireland) and Jim Baker, both Y.M.C.A. mobile canteen workers whose truck had been captured by the Afrika Korps, and some six or so other prisoners, would meet in a quiet corner of the camp to learn from a man who had so much to give – but only because he had himself so obviously received so much from the God he so faithfully served. It was a privilege to sit at his feet and I shall always thank God for every remembrance of him. He died in 1981. After we had been meeting and studying together for several months, Douglas told us one day that we ought to test how much we had learnt. He suggested that he would write to the Methodist Church in England and ask them to send him some copies of the Methodist Lay Preachers' Examination paper – in a very much simplified form for wartime use – and that those of us who wanted to should sit for this exam, properly invigilated by Douglas himself. He would then post the papers we had completed back to England. This we did, using one of the huts in the camp as the examination room. The papers were collected up by Douglas and sent off.

Weeks passed and I had almost forgotten about the exam, when one day, to my surprise and delight, I received in the post a little slip of paper informing me that I had passed and therefore now qualified as a Methodist Lay Preacher! It turned out to be a spectacular bit of timing on God's part, for a few days later we heard over our secret radio that Allied Forces had landed on the Italian mainland and as they fought their way up through Southern Italy hopes ran high in the camp that we might soon be released. On 8th September we heard the news that the Italians had capitulated. Our sentries either disappeared completely, or suddenly became very friendly and came in and mingled with the prisoners. The Italian Colonel who had been in charge of the camp informed the Officers and Warrant Officers that we were not yet out of the wood however, and that it would be extremely dangerous to do anything that might draw the attention of the German forces, now streaming nose to tail in endless conveys along every road leading to the fighting zone, to the existence of the camp. From what he said, the Germans were in a very ugly mood. Escaping prisoners of war were being shot. Italian soldiers were being treated as deserters, rounded up and marched off under conditions of savage cruelty to work in German labour camps. The country was being systematically denuded of all livestock, food, machinery and anything else that might be of use to the German war effort. A patrol of our own men, sent out to try to verify these facts, soon returned to confirm a great deal of what the commandant had said. It was obviously going to be touch and go which forces reached us first, Allied or German.

In spite of this, a great thanksgiving service was conducted by Padre Thompson and the other chaplains on 9 September. I remember we sang Psalm 126 which begins: "When the Lord turned again the captivity of Sion then were we like unto them that dream. Then was our mouth filled with laughter and our tongue with joy." It was all woefully premature. Six days later German motor-cycle troops of the 5th Panzer Division threw a cordon round the camp and we watched with a sense of foreboding as steel helmeted German soldiers climbed up into the machine-gun towers. We had ceased being *prigionieri di guerra*; we were now *Kriegsgefangeners*.

Some of the men who had been captured more recently and had not endured the rigours of the Libyan transit camps were fit enough to make a run for it and a number got away.

Those of us who had arrived as physical wrecks from the Libyan camps and had really had little chance to build up our strength were in the main realistic enough to accept the fact that walking to freedom, even if possible for the few, was out of the question for us. Some were too weak to walk a mile, let alone several hundred. Yet for an all too brief moment freedom had seemed very near – it was a bitter disappointment and very hard to take.

The next day different troops took over from those of the Panzer Division, and the first batch of prisoners was detailed off for evacuation to Germany. My turn came a day later and a further batch of about a thousand men were marched out of the camp down to the railway station at Porto San Giorgio, loaded onto metal cattle trucks and locked in. Each truck had a bucket in it for use as a lavatory, and occasionally on the long train journey up through the Udine Pass into Germany, the train halted long enough for the men to be allowed out, one truckload at a time, to relieve themselves by the railway track under the watchful eyes of the armed German guards and the muzzles of the machine guns mounted at intervals on the roofs of the trucks – partly, I suspect, as anti-aircraft protection, but also to ensure that no prisoner would think he might have a chance if he made a dash for it. Most of the five or six days and nights we spent in the train we could see nothing, but we were very aware of trains passing us at short and regular intervals going in the opposite direction. Whenever we were allowed out, however, we could see that train loads of troops, tanks and guns were pouring south down into Italy and that for the time being at any rate the Allied thrust northwards was being held – a fact which only added to our depression. Eventually we felt the train stop and then the trucks were shunted for some distance along what seemed to be a long siding till they came to a halt once again. Keys were turned in the locked doors and German guards thumped on the side of the trucks as they slid the doors open. Amidst shouts of "*Raus mensch*"[1], we climbed down to stand for the first time on the soil of the Fatherland.

1 An abbreviation of Heraus – Get out.

## CHAPTER SEVEN

# A Hell of a Place!

THE PRISON CAMP into which we were herded was a depressing, grim looking place, and not just because of the double fence of barbed wire which, together with machine-gun towers, surrounded the empty, half-derelict huts. We had expected that part of the scene. But there was also a sense of death and decay, an awful sadness, that seemed to permeate the place. It was called *Jacobstahl* and, as the name implied, had been a Jewish extermination camp. The poor Jews had long since departed, both from the camp and no doubt from this mortal life. That first night we thought that we were now the only residents – all seemed so totally quiet and still. We slept that night – or tried to – lying on the floor or on the wooden shelves that had been provided for the Jews as beds. Dawn, however, awoke us to a still more terrible scene. In a part of the camp separated by an internal nine foot high wire fence from the huts we were occupying, ghastly skeleton-like figures could be seen shambling about, dressed in rags, bare feet thrust into rough wooden clogs, shaven headed, eyes sunk deep in skull-like faces. The men of the Afrika Korps we had fought against, yet respected, seemed suddenly to belong to a different nation from the one we were in now. These poor souls, dying on their feet before our eyes, were Ukrainians – soldiers captured by the German army as it advanced into Russia. When the British soldiers saw the plight of these poor starving Russians, carefully hoarded stores of food from our Red Cross parcels began to be lobbed over the dividing wire quite spontaneously by a long line of British soldiers to the Russians waiting gratefully to catch them on the other side. The German guards were furious and could not understand why we should want to do such a thing. As armed sentries drove the British back from the wire on one side, and clubbed the Russians back into their huts on the other, a German officer said to us "don't waste good food on these – they are *unter-mensch* (sub-human)"! Such was our introduction to Nazi Germany.

There before our eyes we saw the awful 'Master Race' doctrine of Nazism being put into practice. I had joined the Territorial Army during the pre-war Czech crisis out of a young man's rather idealistic sense of patriotism, but even so, I had never felt very happy with any thought that there could ever be such a thing as a 'just war'. Many times since those wartime years convinced pacifists – whose views I can respect, but not share – have done their best to persuade me that, as a christian minister, I ought to feel a sense of guilt for having once fought as a soldier. I can only say that I have pride, not guilt, at having had an opportunity of sharing in the destruction of something that I now knew to be wholly evil – a far greater evil than war, evil though that may be in itself – for it sought to enslave the minds and bodies and souls of men by means of a greater tyranny than the world had ever known before! If ever a war could be described as a 'just war', I knew then, as I watched those dying Russians, and as I later saw in even worse atrocities, mine was most certainly that.

Thankfully our stay in *Jacobstahl* was only brief and a few days later we were transferred to a huge, almost city-like, transit camp *Stammlager IVb*. I have been told that at that time it held forty thousand prisoners – men, and a few Russian Women Medical Officers – of many different nations. There were French, Dutch, Russians and Poles, besides the British, and of course plenty of German guards both outside and inside the camp. The French had been there the longest and were therefore well established and highly organised. Their part of the camp reminded me of pictures I had seen of some of the Wild West frontier towns of 19th century America with their dirt roads, beer halls, cooking houses and canteens. There was even a library! It was they who virtually ran the internal workings of the camp. But here too the dreadful racist hierarchy of the Nazi 'master race' philosophy was made visible. At the top of the ladder came the arrogant, bullying guards. The British, probably only because they represented an as yet unconquered race, came next. The French, Dutch and other prisoners of German occupied Europe came on the rungs lower down. But right at the bottom, held in a separately wired off part of the camp, were the Russians, who did all the filthiest, most degrading jobs in the camp and when not actually working, stood around in the mud of their compound – thin, listless figures like the ones we had seen in *Jacobstahl*. I can remember seeing and hearing the British soldiers infuriating the German guards almost to shooting pitch when they booed at the sight of twenty or so Russian prisoners straining like overladen mules on long ropes as they pulled a heavy sewage cart through the camp under the command of a French prisoner. I'm afraid that in those impetuous days of our youth we blamed and reproached the French for what seemed to us their overwillingness to collaborate with the Germans. Later, as I met many other men from countries that had been overrun and occupied – Czechs, Poles, Dutch and others – I began to understand how very much harder it was for those whose wives, parents and other loved ones were living under the harsh regime of the Nazi conquerors, than it was for us. Now, looking back on those days, far from being judgmental towards those who took the line of least resistance, I can only be the more amazed at the courage and devotion of those who, at enormous risk to themselves and their families, joined the various resistance groups in all the occupied countries and fought – and often died – rather than accept enslavement.

Gradually the Germans sorted out the prisoners and allotted them to their various groups for dispatching to other camps – officers to *Offlags* – other ranks to Work Camps. The Chaplains, because they carried Officers' rank, were sent off to *Offlags*, which meant that I had to say goodbye to Padre Douglas Thompson. I did not see him again until after the war. Strangely enough, although it was not permitted for Padres to go with the other ranks, Medical Officers were sent to each of the *Stalags*. Perhaps the Germans felt that whereas a Doctor might be expected to keep the men fit enough to work for the Glorious Third Reich, a Padre might help to keep the men's spirits up too much and thus encourage resistance! That would never do. They wanted cringing beaten slaves in their slave labour force, not men who marched to work whistling and with a firm unshakable faith that it would only be a matter of time before Germany would be *Kaputt*! They found the British prisoners a great disappointment.

A group of about a dozen of us had done our best to stick together since leaving P.G.70, but when I heard that all of them had been detailed to go off in one of the parties and that men with the rank of corporal and over were to remain in camp, I decided that I was not going to be left behind. I removed my two stripes and a crown (my regiment, the Middlesex Yeomanry, still used the old cavalry badges of rank) and wangled myself on to the party. For one thing, I felt that the possibility of escape might well be better in some small work camp than in the huge well guarded *Stammlager* and wondered if perhaps we might be going to work on some nice, peaceful farm somewhere deep in the countryside! After a long journey – via a thousand bomber raid by the R.A.F. on Leipzig on the way – we arrived at a prison camp, one of a great string of similar camps housing men of many nations, alongside a huge oil refinery, the *Hermann Goering Benzin Fabrik* – at Brux, near Chemnitz (now called Karl Marx Stadt), on the Czechoslovakian border. Any ex-R.A.F. or U.S.A.F. Bomber Command men will easily find it for you on a map. It was one of their regular targets! Theresienstadt concentration camp, where 50,000 Jews were being worked to death or gassed, was only a few miles away – a small camp compared with Auschwitz over the Polish border! There, five million Jews were dying, together with brave men and women of many nations who had dared to resist the might of Nazi Germany.

## CHAPTER EIGHT

# Stalag IVa

THE CAMP WAS SMALL compared with these we had known in Italy and more recently in Germany. Our new Camp Commandant had, I noticed, an Iron Cross first class, which at any rate suggested that he, and the troops guarding us, were front line troops, not just prison guards, and might be expected to treat us with a bit more respect than some we had had to put up with. Perhaps we even hoped they might prove to be more like the Afrika Korps we had known in the desert. Soon after we had settled into the row of wooden huts, we were ordered out to be addressed by the Commandant. He told us that we would be marched each day to the Oil Refinery. We would be expected to work for twelve hours each day except Sunday and anyone found attempting to escape would be shot. He gave various other instructions on behaviour in the camp and while out on work parties. We had with us one officer – a very fine Scottish Medical Officer – and two sergeants who were to be responsible for the discipline of the camp from the British side. These three then said to the Commandant that since the *Benzin Fabrik* was obviously a war factory it was against the Geneva Convention that prisoners of war should be made to work there. In reply the Commandant tapped the luger automatic at his belt and said "This is my Geneva Convention – you will work, and if you do not go to work tomorrow we will take five men and put them against that wall and shoot them – and the next day, five more – and so on, until you do".

We went back to our huts worried, but not unduly so. We thought the Germans were just bluffing. We didn't yet appreciate that most of the troops around us were not like those we had fought in the desert. We were now behind the German lines on the Russian front and most of the troops around us were embittered, war-hardened men who had seen action, endured terrible hardships, and seen many atrocities in the total war that was being fought on that front.

We were also yet to learn that the Gestapo was very much in evidence throughout the factory itself, with its agents and spies everywhere, and that the ordinary German soldier was almost as frightened of the Gestapo and the S.S. as was the civilian population. That evening the road past the camp filled with men of almost every European nation – French, Dutch, Czechs and Poles in particular – trudging back from the factory to their various camps under German guards. The whole place was run with the help of a huge international slave labour force of which we had suddenly and forcibly become a part. It was they who assured us that the Germans were not bluffing, that men had indeed been shot in other camps for refusing to work, and that we would certainly have men shot if we attempted to resist. After a formal protest, we went to work next morning, as there seemed little point in putting lives at risk by doing otherwise.

The Refinery was vast. It was one of many establishments built in coal mining areas such as the area around Brux, in which coal was processed to produce oil and petrol to help to keep the Nazi war machine running. As such it was necessarily high on the Allies' target list for their bombers. In daylight, the U.S.A.F. would come with massed formations of Flying Fortresses and bomb along the wide valley in which the refinery lay. The R.A.F. – and occasionally single bombers we believed to be Russian – bombed us by night. The R.A.F. was very accurate and usually sent Pathfinder Mosquitoes ahead to mark out storage tanks, gasometers and vital buildings with coloured flares. Minutes later we would hear the deep rumbling growl of the heavy bombers. I don't know which we most feared, for though we did our best to cheer the bombers patriotically (mainly to infuriate the German guards!), we still feared for our lives, and casualties were heavy.

If the *Luft gefahr* (air raid warning) sounded when you were at work in the factory, there was really nothing you could do but sprint as fast as you could for one of the coal mines and get underground if possible. The Germans had huge concrete bunkers to go to, which were pretty well bomb proof. The prisoners and civilian slave labour force had only open trenches in which to shelter. True, these could give you a certain amount of protection from blast and shrapnel, but when overhead pipes and storage tanks ruptured in the bombing, these trenches became filled with blazing oil and petrol. You could either stay on the surface and get blown to bits, or shelter in a trench and be burnt to bits! We lost thirty-eight men in one raid alone. It was a miracle there were not more.

Quite apart from the bombs, the falling shrapnel was another very real hazard. There was a huge number of anti-aircraft guns around the refinery. They were of all calibres, from large guns mounted on railway trucks, to quick firing heavy machine guns. When the bombers came over the site they flew into what must have been a hail of bullets and shells. This was especially true of the American Fortresses which came in quite low to drop their bombs all together in one great carpet of destruction. Let no one doubt the courage of those young American airmen! When they arrived over us they had already fought their way across Germany without fighter cover, and no doubt under attack from German fighters most of the way. Over the target area, even though that would be blotted out by what the Germans called *nebel*1 at ground level, the planes were clearly visible in the sights of every gunner on the ground. As they entered the barrage we would see two or three of these great planes begin to wheel slowly out of the formation, some already trailing plumes of smoke behind them and spin to earth. The rest of the formation would move up to plug the gaps and continue on with the bombing run. Then the survivors had to fight their way back across hostile country to their own bases again. Brave men indeed!

It was the 'carpet bombing' of the Americans which caused most casualties among the prisoners, but this was only because their raids were in daytime when we would be digging trenches in the refinery area, or else unloading pig-iron or railway sleepers in the railway yards. But if the 'Yanks' caused most casualties, it was certainly the R.A.F. heavy bombers (and their very heavy bombs!) that did the most damage. Yet we were not all that well disposed towards the Royal Air Force either,

1 A chemically produced fog

for all their accuracy. They had a practice of dropping a load of 'D.A.' (delayed action) bombs, as well as leaflets written in German telling us that the bombs might go off at any time in the next week or so. Somebody back home obviously had the mistaken idea that the Germans would say "Oh dear, how very dangerous! We must clear the area and close down the *Fabrik* at once." Not a bit of it! Life was cheap in Germany and slave labour plentiful. We were back at work next day as usual, the only difference being that there would be large unexploded bombs all over the place, down holes or with fins sticking up out of the ground, which might explode at any moment. No, the R.A.F. were not too popular at times.

The strains and stresses of the bombing, added to the hardships and privations of P.o.W. life brought home to me the spiritual vacuum we were in. As I have pointed out, there was no Padre to minister to the men and it was pretty obvious that such a ministry was desperately needed. The little scrap of paper I had brought with me from Italy telling me I was a Lay Preacher began to burn a hole in my pocket and challenge me accusingly! It seemed to be saying to me: "It's got to be you or no one. What are you going to do about it?" I finally accepted the challenge – very unwillingly at first, I may say! – and went to see the German Commandant. I showed him my bit of paper and said: "Look, I am not a Padre, but I do have authority to conduct Church Services. Will you give permission for me to start Camp Services next Sunday?" After a good deal of questioning as to what would be done and said, permission was granted. The first morning service was announced for the following Sunday.

## CHAPTER NINE

# The Church of Captivity

AS SOON AS the announcement of Sunday services was made there was an immediate and enthusiastic response. Carpenters in the camp used wood from the Red Cross Packing cases to make an altar we could set up for our worship in the large dining hut each Sunday. Fred Adams, a Guardsman who had been a professional artist before the war, got a supply of paint from the Germans and painted it so well that it really did look as if it had a richly embroidered frontal! You had to get very close to see that it was all just paint. We made a couple of wooden candlesticks and a large wooden cross which we painted gold, to stand on the altar. Our 'Organist and Choirmaster' (the organ was a piano-accordion, but he did play it remarkably well!) got together a fine male voice choir who took pride in singing a well practised anthem almost every Sunday – no mean feat when you are made to work twelve hours a day, six days a week, and hard manual work at that. We were of all denominations and plenty who just had C. of E. on their identity discs but who had never actually darkened the door of a church in their lives! There was a dearth of hymn books and no prayer books at all, except for the one I had brought with me from Italy, together with a Y.M.C.A. publication with the title *Hymns and Prayers for Men in Camp*. I still have it as a cherished memento of the 'Church of the Captivity'. On the first Sunday the dining hut was packed. With a battered Prayer Book, a Bible of which I had very little knowledge, and no training whatsoever in how to lead worship, I stood there feeling totally inadequate and ill-equipped,

LAGERKOMMANDIERTE

STW

Kr. Gef. Nr.: 258103

Bar.: 17 Zimmer: 98

Name: GREAVES

Vorname: D R

Stempel der Firma: PREDIGER

"Prediger" card.

to conduct my first church service! The good Lord must have been very patient with that first amateurish attempt because the congregation returned again the following Sunday and increased in size as the weeks and months went by.

The Germans eventually recognised officially that the Camp Church existed by writing on my works card, which all prisoners had and on which the hours worked were recorded, the word *Prediger* (Preacher). I was also allowed to go under armed escort to visit a nearby American camp. The prisoners there had heard through contacts made with British prisoners in the Refinery that we had regular Church services in our camp. They therefore made a request to their German Commandant that 'the British Padre' should come and conduct a service for them as well. There was of course no Padre – only a *Prediger*! But I was allowed to go.

I went, with an armed German escort of course, not knowing what to expect in the way of reception from the Yanks, who after all were expecting to see a fully qualified British Army Chaplain, but when I got there and explained the situation they were almost overwhelmingly welcoming and grateful. However, I very quickly realised that the sermon I had prepared for them was quite inadequate to meet their needs and would only sound trite and unworthy. These were men who had only been captured very recently. Consequently they were still going through that very real shock and trauma that we too had all had to go through in the early days of our captivity. They had not yet received any mail from home. They had no razors to shave with, nor other things that most of us so easily assume to be necessities, like tooth-brushes, toothpaste and towels. Also, because the normal living standards in the American Army were so much higher than in ours, the privation of prisoner of war life came very much harder to them than to us – and remember we had had plenty of cases of 'barbed-wire-itis' and even suicides in the early days.

I was shown into one of the huts, to find there a large group of men, some white, some coloured, sitting on the floor mostly – there were few chairs – backs to the walls, legs stretched out in front of them, unshaven, painfully thin, a look of despair and hopelessness in their eyes. I could almost hear them saying as I stood in front of them: "Is there any word from the Lord for us? Is there anything you can say in His Name that could meet our need?" We sang together some of their favourite hymns, we prayed together for our loved ones back home, for peace, for each other, and for ourselves, but when it came to the point in our worship when I had planned to give a short address, I was at a total loss. Then one particular Bible passage that I had read one day suddenly came back to me. It had seemed to speak in a very relevant way to my circumstances as a P.o.W. and I'm sure that it was brought to my memory as God's answer to the silent cry for help I had been praying from the moment the service had began. I don't suppose many would expect to find much inspiration in the book Deuteronomy – nor do I imagine for those who are reading these words sitting in the comfort of their own homes, well fed, well clothed and warm, there would seem to be much that was all that special about them. Yet the plain fact is that in a prison camp, behind barbed wire, there were many such passages that came to life for us in a completely new way, and which related with an extraordinary vividness to the conditions in which we found ourselves. This was the passage:

"Thou shalt remember all the way which the Lord thy God led thee these forty years in the wilderness, to humble thee and to prove thee . . . and He humbled thee and suffered thee to hunger . . . that He might make thee know that man doeth not live by bread alone, but by every word that proceeds from the mouth of the Lord doth man live . . . Thou shalt also consider in thine heart that, as a man chasteneth his son, so the Lord thy God chasteneth thee. Therefore thou shalt keep the commandments of the Lord thy God, to walk in His ways and to fear Him. For the Lord thy God bringeth thee into a good land . . . a land wherein thou shalt eat bread without scarceness . . . When thou hast eaten and art full, then shalt thou bless the Lord thy God for the good land which He has given thee. Beware that thou forget not the Lord thy God, . . . lest when thou hast eaten and art full, and hast built goodly houses and dwelt therein . . . then thine heart be lifted up and thou forget the Lord thy God which brought thee forth from the house of bondage". *Deut Ch 8.*

Well, I don't imagine many would find that passage all that moving today, but by the time we had read it through it had reduced many of those American soldiers to tears. I remember one young coloured soldier saying to me "Gee, that might 'a been us!" Indeed it might. And not surprisingly really. We too easily forget that a lot of the bible, both Old and New Testaments, was written by and for people who were in captivity, either as exiles and slaves in Egypt or Babylon, or in Roman prisons.

As Camp *Prediger* it was also my sad privilege from time to time to conduct the burial services. Those who died – mostly as a result of the bombing – were buried in a small military cemetery not far from Brux. In the middle of the cemetery there was a small chapel, though we never made use of it, which I was told had been built by Serbian prisoners during the first World War. The Germans treated us very correctly, as far as funerals were concerned. We were always allowed to march an escort and pall bearer party to attend the service and were also allowed to take a bugler to sound the Last Post. The German escort guards always stood to attention as this was done. In the early days we were allowed coffins for the dead. Towards the end of the war this was not always possible and we had to wrap the bodies in black paper. The first daylight raid by the American Fortresses caused heavy casualties, not only among the British prisoners but among the French and Dutch as well. We lost thirty-eight men in that one raid. It had, of course, to be a mass burial and because it was the first American raid, the Germans made a really big thing of it. Not only were there coffins, there were wreaths of flowers, a firing party of German soldiers to fire a salute over the coffins, a French P.o.W. orchestra to play suitable music, and the *Oberst* (Colonel) in charge of the area made a long speech to us about the terrible deeds of the American terror-bombers! They were always doing their best to drive a wedge between us and the Americans. All the German Camp Commandants attended. Even the S.S. and the Gestapo were represented. The local German news agency – or maybe they were military photographers – took many photographs of the proceedings.

There were three funeral services held, one after the other. A French Army Chaplain conducted a Roman Catholic Service for all the Catholic dead. A Dutch Chaplain conducted a Dutch Reformed Church Service, and I conducted the Church of England Burial Service. About three weeks after this incident I was called to the Camp Commandant's

*The Mass P.o.W. funeral after the first Flying Fortress raid on Brüx. The Oberst and some of the German Camp Commanders*

office. I went, wondering what it was that I had said or done that could have led to such a summons. To my surprise, when I got there he presented me with a full set of the photographs which had been taken at that Service. You will find them in this book. Notice the little Serbian Chapel in the background. Notice too how very camera conscious the *Oberst* was! He is the rather Goering-like figure posing for his picture behind the rows of coffins. The photo of all the various local Camp Commandants may look like a 'still' from the Colditz film! But believe me, these were no play-actors.

*British, French, Dutch and some Italian P.o.W.s killed in the first American day-light raid on Brüx.*

*DRG conducting a burial service. The bugler stands behind ready to sound the Last Post.*

*The French P.o.W. orchestra ready to play music at the mass funeral. To the left of the picture can be seen the German Army detachment.*

*The British contingent. Two Senior Warrant Officers and the Medical Officer are in the centre of the front row.*

*Italian P.o.W.s in the foreground. Fifty-two coffins can be counted in this picture. There were more off the picture on either side.*

*The Oberst prepares to make his Anti-American speech.*

*French Prisoners during the Roman Catholic Service.*

*German Officers placing wreaths before the British coffins.*

*The Oberst with the first World War Serbian Chapel behind him*

## CHAPTER TEN

# Fighting Back

FOR YOU THE WAR IS OVER seems to have been a stock phrase used by their German captors to many prisoners of war at the time of capture. No doubt the Germans hoped and thought that would be so! The British, however, never accepted that fact. For them the war would only be over when it was won, and until that happy day came they would continue to fight back in whatever way was open to them. I have already said in an earlier chapter that the Nazi 'Master Race' philosophy meant, among other far worse things, that they wanted the prisoners of war to look cowed and beaten. British prisoners knew this perfectly well and fought back with a deliberate propaganda war. Precious cigarettes and chocolate from Red Cross parcels were used to barter with the Czech civilians for boot polish and metal polish. When the men were called out in the early morning to parade for work, they fell in on right hand markers as if on a parade ground at home, clean-shaven, with boots and buttons shining and uniforms pressed. When they set off to work it was at a brisk march, with arms swinging and heads held high. Once clear of the camp the whistling would start, usually at the head of the column – and the German guards would rush forward with their rifles and bayonets at the ready to stop it. As they neared the front ranks it would fade away and start at the back! After fruitless attempts to stop it they usually gave up, and the whole column, including the German guards, would go swinging through the Czech villages to the strains of "We're going to hang out the washing on the Siegfried Line . ." or some other equally provocative ditty! It was a magnificent gesture of defiance, and the Germans both hated it, yet in some way admired it too.

The Red Cross Food parcels were themselves a great help in this propaganda war. The Germans for example had not seen, smelt or tasted real coffee for years. The only coffee they had had was a dreadful *ersatz* concoction made from ground roasted acorns. It might have looked like coffee, but it had no smell and tasted vile. We used to be given a cupful of it early in the morning before setting off to work.

The Canadian Red Cross parcels, however, always contained a tin of real ground coffee, which gave off that strong and unmistakable aroma and, whenever possible, would be drunk with every display of enjoyment upwind of the nearest German sentry! Chocolate and cigarettes were similarly flaunted. In this way we felt that we were giving clear signals to the German soldiery around us, that our nation continued to be rich and prosperous whatever their own propagandists might tell them, and that should bribes be needed, we had items to offer which they might well secretly covet. On both counts we were to be proved right.

I have already mentioned that we were expected to work six days a week, but Sunday was a day of rest. That was not always the case! Sometimes we would be fast asleep in our bunks on a Sunday morning enjoying, as we thought, a well earned lie-in, when suddenly the hut door would be kicked open by a jack-booted guard shouting "*Raus mensch! Arbeit! Schnell, Schnell*"[1] We of course would protest and point out that we didn't work on Sunday, but the guard would insist: "Today", he would say "is a special day for Hitler; the German people work today for Hitler; *you* must work today for Hitler!" And off we were marched very unwillingly to work. The British soldier being what he is, it wasn't long before some started saying "Blow this for a lark" – or words to that effect! "If we've got to do extra days for Hitler, I'm bloody well taking a day off for Churchill!" So grew the practice known on both sides of the wire as "doing a Churchill". Almost every day there would be one or two – very occasionally three, though that was pushing your luck a bit! – who would hide away somewhere in the camp, perhaps under the floor boards, up in the roof or in some dark corner, with the intention of dodging a day's work.

1 "Get up! To work! Quickly, quickly!"

The rest of us became past masters in the art of concealing their absence by means of a moving blank file as we were counted out of the gate. This was a form of 'goon-baiting', as we called it, that drove the German guards into a frenzy, and the *Feldwebel* (C.S.M.) in charge dangerously near to shooting point sometimes. They would count the men on parade and either come up with the wrong figure or possibly detect some slight movement that made them suspicious, and the count would begin again. This might well produce a different figure, so they would try again! Sometimes departure would be delayed for the best part of an hour before they were satisfied, either that no one was missing – in which case the doer of 'the Churchill' might well get away with his day of rest, provided he stayed hidden and had remembered to take both food and water with him into his hiding place – or else guards would be sent off to search the camp for the missing man or men. It was a dangerous business 'doing a Churchill' because the search by the guards would be no kid gloved affair and they were prone to prod into likely places with bayonets. To be discovered would mean a beating up before being taken off to the 'cooler', or punishment cell, for a few days. In spite of the dangers, the practice continued, and every morning as we paraded the Camp Commandant would wag his finger at us and say "Today there vill be no Churchills". I'm sure Mr. Churchill himself would have been very proud if he had known how his name was taken – and not in vain!

At work in the refinery, acts of sabotage were occasionally possible, but could only be undertaken with extreme care. Not only did we have armed German guards with us, but usually German or Czech *Obermeisters* (Foremen), many of them also armed. They would be continuously screaming at us to work harder since we invariably stopped work and leaned on our shovels the moment their backs were turned. We did however manage to put sand into the bearings of some of the railway trucks in the railway yards when we worked there. Whether it achieved anything it was impossible to say, and we were always conscious that innocent Czech railwaymen and their families might well be accused and punished if our acts of sabotage were discovered.

One of the factors that made the possibility of escaping so remote in that area was that you just could not trust the civilian population. Some of the Czechs were openly collaborating with the Nazis and many who weren't were understandably too scared to admit it. On one occasion we had a Czech foreman over us who seemed worse than the Germans in his apparent hatred of us. All day long he would rant and rave and shout at us for not working enough – under the protection of the German armed guard, needless to say. But one day some of us had got him alone, away from the sentry who had gone to speak to another German soldier a few yards away, and we asked him why, since we had no quarrel with Czechoslovakia, he hated the British so much. Looking around him with a great fear in his eyes he whispered, "I *don't* hate you. But you are prisoners of war. You won't work unless I make you. If I don't make you work, nothing will happen to me, but one day the Gestapo will come, and they will say to me "your wife and daughter live at such and such an address don't they? You wouldn't like anything to happen to them, would you? – so see that you get more work out of these men". A courageous man can be very brave when his own life is threatened. It is not so easy when you know that those you love might be thrown into a German brothel, or a concentration camp, if you displeased your country's invaders. The Nazi knew how to use to the full this kind of terror.

Another dreadful example of Nazi tyranny at its worst could be seen on most days when we were taken to work at the Refinery. This was what we called the 'E gangs'. These were gangs of men, and women, with shaven heads, the thinnest of clothing even in the coldest of winter days – rough wooden clogs stuffed with dirty old rags on their feet, dirty, gaunt and painfully thin, and each with a large 'E' painted on their backs. Where they came from I never discovered, but I imagine it must have been from one of the nearby concentration camps. The male S.S. guards carried long wooden clubs with which they constantly belaboured their frail and helpless men prisoners. The women guards in charge of the women prisoners carried long leather whips, also freely used. These poor wretches were made to carry heavy railway sleepers and do other very heavy work – and do it almost at a run, though you wondered how such spindly legs could stand, let alone run. If one of them dropped to the ground they would be brutally kicked and beaten until they either staggered to their feet again, or were found to have taken the only possible escape route from the hell they were in, in which case another ragged scare-crow would be driven over with a wheelbarrow to load up the corpse, presumably to be taken back to their camp and thrown into a lime pit, as we had seen Russian prisoners do at Jacobstahl. And this was not done in secret, but out in the wide streets which ran through the middle of the refinery, in full view of the office windows where young German typists sat at their typewriters and filing clerks kept the office records. I have never found it easy to believe it when, after the war, I met many Germans who told me that they had no idea what was going on in their country. Some, perhaps, in remote country districts, may genuinely have been ignorant of the enormity of the crimes against humanity which were being perpetrated by their country's Nazi regime. I can only be quite sure that those who lived in the area of Brux could

*"E" gang at work at Brüx*

not claim any such ignorance. It was going on before their eyes.

I can remember too an occasion when we were being marched as usual to work and a small German lorry overtook the column and then, because of other traffic, had to slow down just ahead of us. The back of the lorry was open and standing in it against the tailboard we were surprised and delighted to see a group of pretty young women together with a black-uniformed German guard. Soldiers have never been backward at expressing their appreciation at the sight of the fair sex, so not surprisingly the whole column began cheering, giving wolf whistles, and waving to the girls. They, who at first had looked pale and drawn, smiled and started to wave back – one even, perhaps unwisely, gave the 'V for Victory' sign, and it was then we saw that they were manacled. At once the guard punched her in the face and began slapping her and some of the other girls. The British prisoners almost went berserk. They booed, they shouted, they shook their fists, until the S.S. guard, almost snarling with rage at such blatant disregard for his authority, drew his pistol and looked as if he might well start blazing away at the whole lot of us. Luckily for us – though not, I fear for those poor girls – the obstruction that had been holding up the truck moved out of the way and the driver accelerated on up the road away from us, still pursued by our jeers and boos. Our own sentries had unslung their rifles and had done their best to restrain us and they seemed very fearful as to what repercussions there might be from this incident. I have often wondered who those girls were. Were they members of the Resistance who had been rounded up and were being taken to a concentration camp – or were they possibly some of the amazingly courageous British girls who were parachuted into occupied France and other countries, to work as agents with the resistance? I wonder if any of them survived. I shall never know, but I remember spending almost the whole of the next night praying for God to give them courage and to be very near them, whoever they were.

Before I leave this chapter, which has had a good deal to say about the evils of Nazism, I must just add this. I have often been asked if, because of my experiences, I have been left with a hatred of the German people in my heart. My honest answer is no, not in the least. I have some very good friends who are Germans. Nor do I forget that there were many Germans who were themselves sent to concentration camps and to torture and death because they could not and would not be a part of what they saw to be evil. I have no hatred of the German people. I can admire the skill of a Boris Becker, Wimbledon Tennis Champion at 18, or the graceful loveliness of a Katerina Witt, five times World Champion in Ice Figure Skating, as much as any man. But I do have a great hatred for Nazism and all it stood for.

## CHAPTER ELEVEN

# For You The War Was Over

FOR US it went on a bit longer! As in Italy, we still managed to listen to the B.B.C. news, or to find out from outside contacts what was happening. We made maps on which we recorded where the Russian advance had got to on one side of us, and where the American troops had reached on the other. Even without radio news we would have known that the Allied Forces were steadily drawing nearer, from hearing the welcome but often dangerous sound of bombers approaching *before* the air raid sirens started up. You had to respect and even admire the sheer dogged tenacity of the Germans, though. Time after time the bombers would leave the refinery looking just a pile of broken pipes and blazing storage tanks and rubble. Surely, we'd say to ourselves, it's finished now – *kaputt*! they'll never get petrol out of this place again! But within minutes of the all clear sounding, lorry loads of German labour corps troops would drive into the wreckage, arc lights would burn all night – if there were not more air raids – and a couple of days later, they would have the thing churning out petrol again. It was fantastic. We knew that the outcome of the war could now only be victory for the Allies and defeat for Germany, but I think we also had a sneaking feeling that a nation of people who could work like that could not be kept under for long. But to get back to the maps – always when we marked up on them the Russian and American lines, Brux seemed to remain midway between the two. It looked as if it would be a fifty-fifty chance whether we would be released by Uncle Sam or Uncle Joe. Not that we minded too much – as long as *someone* came!

Then came V.E. Day and with it a great sense of relief in the camp. The German Commandant told us that officially the war was over but he regretted that his orders were to keep us confined within the camp and under guard until he was instructed otherwise.

We could still hear the rumble of gunfire not too far away in spite of the official ceasefire, but with the knowledge that there would be no *arbeit* tomorrow, we sat up late that night and talked until the early hours of our hopes and plans for the future. Eventually we turned in and went to sleep, anticipating a good lie-in in the morning. Dawn however brought a very rude awakening. Shells were bursting not all that far away and we could even hear the rattle of small arms fire. We dressed hurriedly and rushed out. As it got lighter, we could see on the high ground towards what was then Chemnitz – now Karl Marx Stadt – all the signs of a heavy battle going on, and the shape of tanks, which we knew could only be Russian, advancing slowly under fire over the hills. All around in the street outside the camp there was sheer panic. Civilians were clinging to all the German military vehicles that were streaming past in an endless line whilst others, pushing hand carts and laden prams, walked and ran along the road in terror. The Sudaten Germans, and those Czechs who had collaborated too freely, had no doubt heard too many German accounts of Russian atrocities to allow themselves to fall into Russian hands if they could possibly avoid it. Nor were the Germans prepared to allow us to fall into Russian hands – though why they were so insistent about that I could never really understand.

Only those in the *Krankenhaus* (sick bay) were left behind; the rest of us were forced out of the camp at gun point to accompany the retreating Germans. We learnt from them that the Russians had pushed up from Chemnitz overnight but that the German troops, many of them S.S., who could expect no quarter from the Russians, were still resisting strongly and holding them back so that as many as possible, both civilians and military, could get away to Karlsbad where, it was hoped they would be able to surrender to the American forces.

Our former prison camp guards had long since ceased to worry about us and had simply melted into the great mass of people surging down every road that might take them away from the advancing Russians.

Eight of us who had stuck together ever since desert days kept walking in the direction everyone else was going, because we had decided that we too would rather fall into the hands of the Americans than the Russians – partly because we knew we could identify ourselves to the Americans rather more easily than to the Russians, but also because we knew that our khaki uniforms, at a distance, might well be mistaken for those of the German labour corps, whose uniform was very similar. We suspected that the Russians might well shoot first and ask questions after! However, it was a very dangerous business to be a British P.o.W. just walking along with the rest. Not all the Germans accepted that they were beaten. Some of the fanatical Nazis were almost beside themselves with rage at what was happening to the *Vaterland* and were quite likely to relieve their feelings by shooting you. I remember seeing a German officer, who looked as if he might have been high on Schnapps, urging a weary, bewildered and scared looking column of very young soldiers – they must have been Hitler Youth, some little more than boys – to sing some of their marching songs and even to goose-step as they marched. He was constantly shouting at them, when he wasn't swearing at any civilians or even other German soldiers who got in their way. Some of the Czechs, in anticipation of the arrival of the Russians, had rather unwisely hung hammer and sickle flags out of the windows of their houses. This was the proverbial red rag to a bull to the Hitler Youth leader, who at once sent some of his lads to pull them down and trample on them if they were in reach, and to smash the ground floor windows if they weren't. On a couple of occasions he lobbed a hand grenade through the window causing a sudden panic-stricken scattering of everyone else in the vicinity until the thing exploded. I'm sure he was either drunk or deranged.

By the time my companions and I had reached the small town of Chomutov we were footsore, weary and hungry. Seeing some faces peering from an upstairs window in a block of Czech workers' flats we stopped and made signs that we would like to come up to see them. The faces disappeared from the window but as we waited, a door leading on to the pavement was cautiously opened and a hand beckoned us to come in. A young man asked who we were and by means of a mixture of German, English and a smattering of French we introduced ourselves, explaining that we were British soldiers from a prison camp at Brux. He led us up a couple of flights of concrete steps into one of the flats where his wife and two other people were waiting to greet us. They invited us to sit down at their table and with great generosity asked us to join them in a meal. I think that after spending some time with our new found friends and the sheer nostalgic pleasure it gave us just to be in an ordinary family home again, we had almost decided to stay there and sit it out until the Russians arrived. A sudden crash of glass and the shouting of German voices quickly changed our minds. We looked out of the window to see German soldiers setting up anti-tank weapons and machine guns in the ground floor windows, and others preparing to block off the road as soon as the last of the German convoys had passed through. Obviously there was going to be house-to-house fighting in Chomutov and we had no intention of getting caught up in that. Saying a hurried goodbye to our Czech friends, we went down the stairs and into the street again. The German troops scowled at us, but were too busy to bother too much about us, so we made for the half completed road block where the vehicles were having to slow down in order to negotiate it, in the hope that we might be able to hurl ourselves on board one of them. Our feet were too sore to contemplate more walking, except as a last resort. It didn't look very hopeful though. Every vehicle that came along still had people clinging at every possible point, standing on the running boards, and lying on the cab roof. There wasn't an inch to spare. We had almost given up and decided to start walking, especially as the sounds of battle were getting uncomfortably close again, when there came a sudden gap in the endless stream of vehicles, and in the gap came a single open-topped lorry with just two people in it – the driver and one other German soldier! We could scarcely believe our luck and got ready to leap in the back as the lorry approached the road block and slowed down to a crawl. The two Germans saw what we were about to do, but made no attempt to prevent us. We scrambled aboard – and then as the lorry began to pick up speed again we realised why, unlike every other vehicle, it was empty of passengers. It was full of ammunition.

## CHAPTER TWELVE

# Journey's End

IT WASN'T AN IDEAL CHOICE of vehicle at that particular moment. Not only were Russian shells falling in the near distance but there was always the distinct possibility that Russian fighters might come over and strafe the German convoys. Surprisingly, though, we saw no sign of the Russian Air Force throughout the journey. The new hazard was that some of the Czechs were now sniping at the Germans from rooftops, and that worried us a good deal. It seemed ridiculous to get blown up after a war was over! Thankfully, no stray bullets hit us and eventually the lorry drove into the outskirts of Karlsbad, where it stopped. It had to, because from that point on nothing on wheels could move. Karlsbad was jammed solid with people. I don't know how the Germans knew where the demarcation line divided the Russian Zone from the American, but somehow the news had gone around that once they reached Karlsbad they were safe from the Russians. It was literally standing room only. As soon as we jumped off the lorry we were besieged by German soldiers all wanting to surrender to us and offering us their weapons! I didn't much fancy carting a rifle about so I refused all those, but with recent memories of the fanatical Hitler youth leader, and others like him, still roaming free, we all felt it was wise to arm ourselves, so we collected side-arms from German officers and went off to look for the Americans.

We finally found them – or rather him! – for the only American we found was a very harrassed looking motorcyclist standing at the town centre surrounded by a great mass of German soldiers and civilians, all of whom appeared to be shouting at him at once and asking what they should do and where they should go. We forced our way through the crowds and made ourselves known to him. "Can you speak the lingo?" he said. When we said we could – enough to make ourselves understood – he asked if we would try to sort out the traffic snarl-ups that were blocking every road into the city. "Make the vehicles pull off the roads on to the sidewalks or something", he said. We replied that we didn't mind helping out for a bit, but that we wanted first and foremost to make contact with the main American Forces and to get back home as soon as possible. We had no wish to hang about in Karlsbad. "That's not possible right now", he said, "nothing and nobody is to go beyond here. Our troops have set up road blocks from here to where our main forces are, still several miles back, and they've got orders to shoot anyone who tries it. You'll only get yourselves shot if you go further. Better find yourselves somewhere to sleep here tonight".

Finding anywhere to *stand* was problem enough in Karlsbad at that moment! Every building seemed to be crammed with people and we felt that the chances of finding any accommodation were very remote. However, we agreed to go and see what we could do to help for a while, but arranged to meet again afterwards, to decide what to do next. It was while I was doing my bit of traffic policeman duty that a German officer, evidently believing me to have some authority in the town, came and took hold of my arm and begged me, with tears in his eyes, to come and help him. Not knowing what the trouble was, but sensing that it was something urgent and desperate, I agreed to go with him. He led me to the railway station where a train was waiting in the station. As we approached it I could hear men groaning and crying out with pain. The whole train, he told me, was full of badly wounded and dying soldiers from the Russian front, but the train had been stopped there and the driver told it could go no further. He had then got off the train and left them. His men urgently needed medical treatment and he pleaded with me to help him get them to hospital. As gently as I could I did my best to explain to him that I had no authority to do anything and that I doubted whether there was anything that could be done until the American forces arrived with their ambulances, Advance Dressing Stations and Field Hospitals. We both returned to the busy street and asked everyone we met if there was a hospital in the city. I'm sure there must have been, but everyone we asked was as much a stranger in the place as I was and had no idea. Even if we had found one, I suspect it would have already been full to overflowing and it would in any case have been virtually impossible to get the wounded moved there. There was nothing more I could do, other than tell the American motorcyclist about the German wounded and ask him to let his own medical officer know as soon as he could make contact with the main forces. He said he would, but I didn't get the impression that he was all that concerned about the German wounded. I began to realise that probably because I had until very recently been a prisoner, and knew something of the sense of helplessness that that German officer was feeling now, I had more compassion towards the defeated foe that had the troops who had defeated them.

It was now late in the day and my companions and I, after talking over the situation, agreed that we had no desire to remain in overcrowded Karlsbad. In spite of the American's warning, the verdict was to take a chance and 'go and look for the Yanks'. We set off in the most likely direction. Once clear of the town, we went with great caution, mindful of the presence of pockets of Nazi troops which were likely to be around, as well as keeping a careful lookout for American road blocks. Whether we were lucky in the route we had chosen, or whether it was because we deliberately avoided what we thought were likely to be danger spots, we saw no signs of either. But it was getting dark and some of my companions were all for looking now for a farm house and demanding beds and food for the night – at gun point if necessary, since we were all armed. I somehow felt sure that we must be getting close to our goal and was reluctant to give up. "Let's just have a look round the next corner", I said, "and then, if there's still no sign of them we'll lay up somewhere for the night." We walked on the next mile or so to the corner of the road and looked cautiously round it. There, stretching down the road as far as we could see, were tanks, trucks and jeeps of all kinds! Groups of men were sitting by their vehicles. Many more were to be seen in the fields on both sides of the road. They were obviously having a meal – we could smell it, and it smelled delicious! There were no sentries – no one challenged us as we walked towards them. They were, I suppose, relying on their road blocks and on the fact that the war was officially over. We introduced ourselves to the nearest group as being escaping British prisoners of war. They shook us by the hand, saying "have some chow!" and thrust steaming mess-tins full of some sort of meat hash into our very willing hands. In spite of their informality and apparent lack of security, however, somebody must have radioed back to their regimental headquarters and reported our arrival, because about half an hour later an American officer in a jeep drove up and asked each of us in turn our name, number, regiment, and date and place of capture.

*American driver with some of the group who escaped with the author seen here on route for Regensburg*

Strangely enough, the next few days are the ones that I can least well remember of all the three years of my captivity. It all seems a bit hazy somehow. I suppose there was a tremendous emotional upheaval going on in my mind. The very fact that I had survived at all seemed hard to believe, for one thing; the fact that I was really on the way home at last, another. My joy and excitement at the prospect was strangely disturbed too, by the thought of those many friends of mine who had not made it and would never return. On top of the emotional stresses, the rich American food proved more than my weakened inside could take, and

*German prisoner under American guards clearing bomb damage at Regensburg.*

for the first few days of freedom I began to wonder if my old enemy of dysentery had started up again. Once the Americans had checked out our answers and were satisfied that we were bona fide British troops, they could not do enough for us. They took us first to Regensburg airfield where we found German prisoners with American guards clearing up the rubble, filling in bomb holes and generally working to make it operational again. The ride to Regensburg was in open trucks driven by coloured American soldiers who hurtled down pot-holed roads and round blind corners with a total disregard for safety – either of other road users or of ours! We all confessed, after that journey, that we had thought our last hour had come on more than one occasion. However, we got there, and were told to join the great mass of other ex-prisoners sitting on the grass all round the perimeter of the airfield. It was a boiling hot day too, I remember. All day long, Dakotas were landing, loading and taking off again like aerial taxis, one after the other. Our turn came at last and I made my first ever flight in one of these marvellous old 'work-horses' used by both American and British air forces then and for many years after the war. That took us across Germany and just over the French border. Here we were put on a Red Cross train which carried us in great comfort – and what a great contrast it was to the cattle trucks of past railway journeys! – to Le Havre. Here we found another Dakota, operated this time by an R.A.F. crew, which flew us across the Channel. Every man aboard, I'm sure, had a lump in his throat when we saw the white cliffs of Dover beneath us as we crossed the coast.

We landed somewhere in Kent. Since we were all dressed as Yanks – the Americans having deloused us and removed, and no doubt burnt, our P.o.W. uniforms en route – we were kitted out with brand new uniforms and given leave passes and travel warrants for our journeys home.

My parents had as yet no knowledge that I was safe in England. My mother told me later that on V.E. day, like everyone else in their road, they had decorated the house and had a large Union Jack flying from an upstairs window. As the days and weeks after V.E. day went by, one by one the other families in the road took down their decorations, until at

*P.o.W.s (DRG in Armoured Corps beret) waiting on the perimeter of RegensburgA aerodrome for US Dakota tranpsort planes.*

*Dakota landing at Regensburg.*

*Our party going aboard. Other groups behind can be seen entering another Dakota.*

*Red Cross train en route to Le Harve.*

*Landing from an RAF Dakota 'somewhere in England' all dressed in American uniforms.*

last only my home had the flag flying! My father had rung the War Office several times to see if there was any news but was told that the whole situation up there on the Russian front was very confused and they could tell him nothing. Eventually, but only on the day before I landed back in England, my parents took down their flags and decorations too.

When I got back to the main line station in London, I debated whether I should save time by simply getting on the Northern Line of the Underground and go straight home, or whether the shock of my just suddenly appearing on the doorstep might be too much for my mother if I didn't warn her by 'phone in advance! I decided to find a call box and ring. Even then, when she picked up the 'phone and said "Hello, who is it?", and I replied "It's me – David", I half expected to hear a thump at the other end as she fainted! But she didn't, and by the time I reached home about an hour later, not only was my house decked with flags again – most of the other houses in the street were too!

## CHAPTER THIRTEEN

# Rehabilitation and Reflections

LIKE MANY OTHER ex-P.o.Ws I did not find picking up the threads of my life after the war at all easy. There was a very real cultural shock involved in becoming a civilian again. First there was a fairly long spell of leave, during which my mother, in spite of continuing rationing and shortages, did her best to fill me up with more food in a day than I had seen in a week over the previous three years! Then I had to return to the Army to await the day for my official demobilization – in my case 28th February 1946. In that interim period, to keep us from the boredom of having nothing to do, we were sent to a military camp near Tetbury in Gloucestershire and spent our days spud-picking in the surrounding potato fields. That somewhat humdrum occupation out in the peaceful surroundings of the Cotswolds was itself a strange contrast after the noise, smells, harshness and sudden death of the Brux Refinery. Yet it was still the Army, still the communal life of the barrack room, still part of a fairly close-knit fellowship of young men of around your own age, still obeying orders, with little need to make decisions for yourself. We were all impatient to get out of uniform and to get back to 'civvy-street', but in retrospect I cannot help feeling that far from being the time-wasting period in our lives most of us thought it to be, it probably helped us a good deal. Those last few months helped prepare us mentally for the much more traumatic experience of leaving the Army altogether. Not that I wasted any time there, for it was at Tetbury that I met the girl who was to become my wife! With our three children, seven grandchildren and many friends, both past and present, we happily celebrated our Ruby Wedding in 1988.

The cultural shock of returning to civvy-street was threefold:

The first was the matter of *patriotism*. When the Germans invaded Czechoslovakia a year before World War II broke out, I believed that war had already become inevitable. Like many young men of my generation I joined the Territorial Army out of a very real sense of patriotic duty. A group of us from our Insurance Office went off after work one evening and enlisted at the Duke of York's Headquarters in Chelsea to become Troopers in the Middlesex Yeomanry. This ancient and honourable regiment, otherwise known as 'The Duke of Cambridge's Hussars', had served with considerable distinction at Gallipoli and elsewhere. It was still a Cavalry regiment as far as its first line was concerned, but a second line was then being formed and trained as a Signals regiment to serve as part of an Armoured Brigade, together with three other Yeomanry regiments.1 Like most of the young men of my generation, when war came I went off to serve King and Country with a true patriotic desire to preserve what we saw as a freedom and a way of life worth fighting for, and to defeat an evil regime which threatened to enslave the world. Much of it was youthful idealism, no doubt, but it was very real nonetheless.

As a Prisoner of War, patriotism became if anything even more important. It served to emphasise our total separation from, and rejection of, the way of life of our Nazi captors, whose barbed wire fences and machine gun towers surrounded us on every side. I am reminded of those British expatriates in Colonial days who, often as a loyal duty, went off to make their homes in India, Africa and elsewhere, there so often becoming 'more British than the British' in their determination not to be charged with 'going native'! Tea at four, dinner jackets and evening gowns for dinner (in temperatures over 100°), Christmas pudding with a sprig of holly, specially sent out from the old country, at Christmas lunch – it was somehow madness, 'terribly British', yet more than a little magnificent at the same time. I suppose in our little enforced enclaves in an alien and hostile land we were often a bit like that. The National

1 The 3rd Count of London Yeomanry, the 4th County of London Yeomanry and the 2nd Royal Gloucestershire Hussars

Anthem, though *streng verboten* for prisoners, was sung on every possible occasion, standing rigidly to attention, even at the risk of being clubbed to the ground with rifle butts. When that was made impossible, we sang 'Land of Hope and Glory' instead, roaring out "God who made thee mighty, make thee mightier yet" in proud defiance! And when we sang 'God save the King', we actually meant it. We were still the King's soldiers – and proud of it. The King's Christmas message to his people, heard secretly on the radio and read out in each hut, would be listened to with an almost reverent attention by all. Churchill too, as the great lay leader of the Commonwealth, seemed somehow to personify for us resistance against the enemy, so that "doing a Churchill" was one way by which we did our bit to resist the whole Nazi regime.

We soon found that it wasn't like that in 'civvy street'. I can particularly remember what a shock and disappointment it was for me the first time I went to the cinema after the war. When the film ended and the lights came on, the National Anthem began to be played. I stood rigidly to attention and started to sing the words. I found myself singing a solo! All around me people were putting on coats, lighting cigarettes, beginning to chatter, whilst some, with obvious irritation, waited to get past my motionless figure to get outside and catch the bus home. I felt angry and let down, and began to suspect for the first time that the ideal I had fought and suffered for, and many had died for, was really only a dream – something that had existed only in my mind and would never be a reality. Patriotism seemed almost to have become a dirty word in some circles!

The second part of the cultural shock of those early post-war days was *materialism*. For the previous three years my only possessions had been the ragged and verminous clothes I stood up in, and the few necessary articles such as a drinking mug, a mess tin, a small brewing fire – all made from old Red Cross food parcel tins – and a few luxuries like a razor and a bar of soap received from home. I could pick up and carry in my two hands all my worldly goods – and I had sometimes had to do just that when moved from camp to camp. But after 'de-mob' I found myself in a very different world. In may ways of course, vastly better. Don't misunderstand me – I had no monkish nostalgia for the 'simplicities' of life as a P.o.W. In some ways 'civvy street' seemed like paradise after that.

Yet in other ways it was a paradise that was flawed and far from perfect. There was so much materialism in it. The possession of things seemed so important to may. "Keeping up with the Jones's" was the essential thing and an "I'm alright Jack" attitude towards those less fortunate than yourself seemed all to common. During those harsh years of war, Churchill and other great leaders had spoken of duty, of sacrifice, of caring for one another. Men and women had been prepared to give everything they had, including life itself, in the cause of victory and peace. Now it seemed that there were those who wanted everything, but were prepared to give very little in return. Suddenly, it was no longer fashionable even to use the words 'duty' or 'sacrifice'. Now the talk was all of 'rights' – *my* rights, *my* wage packet, *my* standard of living. All that very real sense of comradeship and of all 'being in the same boat', which had marked those grim years of war – and as much in the air raid shelters and bombed streets of civilian life as in a ship's company, aircrew or regiment – all that seemed suddenly to have vanished into the past and to have been forgotten. Certainly one was tempted to forget the hardship and sorrows and privations, yet the sad truth is that though war is a terrible thing and no one in his senses could ever think or say otherwise, the grimmer experiences the more they seemed able to bring out the best, as well as the worst, in human nature.

The third part of the culture shock on returning to civilian life was *self-sufficiency* – man's proud, arrogant, self-sufficiency, which showed itself in so many ways once peace came. How quickly those churches which were packed with praying people when the doodle-bugs and V2s were falling emptied once that danger was removed! Many people called on God for help in those days of fear and uncertainty. When we crouched in slit trenches or waited for the 'whoosh' of hundreds of bombs from Flying Fortresses to fall onto that Brux oil refinery, then to erupt into deafening explosions and flames of fire all around us I don't recall any of us ever claiming to be atheists. Belief in God is instinctive at moments like that and all of us, in our different ways, prayed. It isn't so easy to deny the existence of God when you know that you may well be standing in His presence in the very next moment! Some might call it 'clutching at straws' or just a reaction of fear. I think that is much too glib and easy an explanation, and this instinct to pray at such moments far too general and widespread for it to be dismissed in such a way. The truth surely is that at times of great stress and danger there comes also an awareness of the deep fundamental truths of life, including the truth that God is, and that He is able to help us in our helplessness. But sadly, men and women in their arrogant self-sufficiency so easily and quickly forget. There is nothing new about that of course. Sinful man has always done that. In that bible passage from Deuteronomy I shared with the American P.o.W.s at Brux, there came the warning: "Take heed lest you forget the Lord your God . . . lest when you have eaten and art full and have built goodly houses and live in them . . . then your heart be lifted up, and you forget the Lord your God." It has always been so easy, when you have food in your belly, and a roof over your head, and a good job to go to and the sun shines overhead – oh, it's so easy then to say "I don't need God; I can get along alright without Him; I can take care of myself." How easy it is to kid ourselves that we're self-sufficient then!

I had returned from the war with a new and much deeper faith in God and an awareness of His call to me to offer my life to Him as an ordained minister. I found the war-weary indifference and complacency of so many of those around me hard to understand and even harder to bear at first. They seemed so blind to what to me seemed so obvious! But once I got to College and met my fellow ordinands, all except one (and he had worked down in the coal mines as a Bevan boy!) straight out the Armed Forces as I was, the trauma of my rehabilitation melted away. I was once again in training for active service – and there is no discharge in this war!

# Epilogue

I have often been asked if my war-time experiences affected my life in any way in the years that followed. My answer could, and can, only be "Yes, totally!" To explain what I mean I must first of all take you back to that appalling hell-camp of Suani-ben-Aden, near Tripoli. In a much earlier chapter I tried to put into words something of the awfulness of life there, with its multitudes of fleas and lice, its total lack of shelter in the bitter cold of desert nights and the disease and weakness and death that threatened our survival as all these factors began to take their toll. I can remember one particular night when I couldn't sleep at all, so I sat all night with my back against a palm tree shivering with cold, with a gnawing, aching emptiness in my stomach which was partly hunger and partly due to dysentery. I was only too well aware of the fleas and lice crawling over my body, yet powerless to do anything about them. I knew I was ill, though I didn't, at that stage, know how very ill I was. For the first time really, I think, I began to have doubts about my own survival and wondered how long I could last in the condition.

Sometime during the night I started praying, I wasn't a particularly religious person at that time. My parents were regular church-goers and I had gone to Sunday School, and later to Church with them but up to the outbreak of war I knew that my Christian faith was little more than 'skin-deep' – the way I'd been brought up, though for that I shall always be very grateful.

But now I was really praying for the first time in my life! Looking back to that moment in later years I have realised that it was a very selfish prayer – simply asking God to give me some sign – some token – that I would survive, and giving Him my promise that if I did, I would do my best to serve Him. Not a very worthy prayer, I fear! – but because it was from the heart, I have no doubt that God smiled at its naivety, and accepted it in spite of its short-comings!

At last I heard the cocks crowing in some Arab encampment not far away and knew that the dawn was breaking. The rising sun would at least dispel the chill of the desert night and warm my aching bones. During the day, while searching for lice and lice-eggs in the seams of my tattered shirt, I suddenly felt in the top pocket of the shirt one of the only two possessions I still had – one was a pipe, though I had no tobacco, – and the other was a small New Testament which a fond aunt had given me when she heard I was going overseas, and which I had carried with me, largely unopened I confess, ever since. Now I took it out and opened it – completely at random, for I knew very little about where to find things in it in those days – and my eyes fell immediately on these words:-

"Beloved, do not be surprised at this ordeal that has come to test you, as though some foreign thing befell you. You are sharing what Christ suffered; so rejoice in it, that you may also rejoice and exalt when His glory is revealed . . . . "Once you have suffered for a little, the God of all grace who has called you to His eternal glory in Christ Jesus will repair, recruit and strengthen you. The dominion is His for ever and ever. Amen."

You will find these words in I Peter Chapter 4 vv12,13 and Chapter 5 vv10, 11. The version I had was one of the early attempts at producing a modern translation and which was known as the Moffat's New Testament. Now, perhaps the words don't sound all that special to you, but for me they came as the very word of God! It was as if there were no other words on the page, and I have no doubt whatsoever that this was God's answer to my prayer, and gave me hope and strength to live through the rest of my time at Suani-ben-Aden and to endure the days battened down in the darkness of the hold of the ship that took us eventually across to Sicily. Then, after that spell in Caserta Hospital, came P.G.70 where I was to meet Padre Douglas Thompson and, because of the experience I have just described, found myself drawn into that little group of men in the camp who wanted, like me, to learn more about the things of God.

That led on to sitting eventually for a Local Preacher's exam and to my receiving, just before we heard the news of the Italian Capitulation, a certificate to say that I had passed. Then came the bitter experience of having our high hopes of freedom shattered as we were re-captured by the Germans and carted off to Germany. At Brux life was again very tough and the deep spiritual need of many very apparent. With no Chaplain to meet those needs, I found myself, very reluctantly at first, almost forced into a ministry, first among the men of Stalag IVa, and later in other camps as well, as the camp *Prediger* or Preacher.

When the war ended and I finally returned home I knew that *Prediger* I had been, and *Prediger* I had to continue to be.

I had never had the slightest idea of being ordained prior to the war and was in fact a clerk in the Royal London Mutual Insurance Society Ltd. in Finsbury Square in London. There were no parsons in the family! However I went to see my Vicar – a dear old saint – Prebendary Dunn, then Vicar of St James, Muswell Hill, and talked over my feelings with him. There were many problems. Even in those days it cost a great deal of money to go to a College or University and my parents were far from being wealthy. Prebendary Dunn however was very helpful and encouraging. He said that if ordination really was God's will for me, He would see me through these problems just as surely as He had seen me through all the perils and pains of my prisoner of war days. He have me a verse of scripture which he said I was to take as God's word to me. It was from the Revelation to St John.

"I have set before you an open door which no man can shut"

Revelation Chapter 3 v8.

So it proved to be! I did my training at the London College of Divinity (Now St. John's College, Nottingham) and was ordained Deacon in 1949. Now after thirty-eight years of ministry as a clergyman in the Church of England which took me to Bayswater, to Bromley, to Orpington, to Billericay and finally to Langdon Hills, Basildon – years which were far too busy for writing books! – I have been able, in this first year of my retirement, to write this book. I have done so first, because I have long wanted to do so, secondly, as a tribute to the courage and patient endurance of all who shared with me the privations and dangers of life as a Prisoner of War, but above all the say 'thank you' to the God who long ago in a flea-ridden patch of desert sand "counted me faithful, putting me into the ministry " (I Timothy I v12)

## Addendum

Taken from the 1939-45 cemetery register - Reprinted 1987

Reproduced with the permission of the Commonwealth War Graves Commission who alone hold the copyright of these registers. I am very grateful to them for giving me the permission. D.R.G.

# PRAGUE WAR CEMETERY
## Index No. CZ.1.

Prague War Cemetery is in fact a British plot adjoining a boundary wall on the north side of the civil cemetery of Olsany, which is on the eastern outskirts of Prague, just under 3 kilometres from the centre of the city, on the main road from Prague to Strasnice, which runs due east from Wenceslas Square. The approach to the War Cemetery is the first turning left from the main road past the entrance gates of the civil cemetery; there is a secondary cemetery to the right of this side road, and the plot will be found to the left from the entrance. The construction of this cemetery was carried out by the Czechoslovak Government, to plans provided by the Commonwealth War Graves Commission, under the terms of the War Graves Agreement of 3rd March, 1949.

Graves were brought into this cemetery from 84 small cemeteries scattered all over Czechoslovakia. Many of those buried here died as prisoners of war. The total of 264 burials in Prague War Cemetery is made up as follows:

| FORCES | NAVY | | ARMY | | AIR FORCE | | MISC. | | TOTALS | |
|---|---|---|---|---|---|---|---|---|---|---|
| | known | unknown | known | unknown | known | unknown | known | unknown | known | unknown |
| United Kingdom | 6 | – | *151 | 2 | 21 | 1 | – | 17 | 178 | 20 |
| Canadian | – | – | 7 | – | 2 | – | – | – | 9 | – |
| Australian | – | – | 2 | – | – | – | – | – | 2 | – |
| New Zealand | – | – | 13 | – | 1 | – | – | – | 14 | – |
| South African | – | – | 13 | – | 6 | – | – | – | 19 | – |
| Indian | – | – | – | – | – | – | – | 1 | – | 1 |
| Polish | – | – | – | – | 8 | – | – | – | 8 | – |
| Entirely unidentified | – | – | – | – | – | – | – | 13 | – | 13 |
| | 6 | – | 186 | 2 | 38 | 1 | – | 31 | 230 | 34 |

*Includes 1 Special Memorial 'C', i.e. bearing the inscription "Buried near this spot".

There is also one UK identified burial form the 1914–18 war buried in this cemetery.